Train Your Own Mini

**To Show in Halter Classes
To Drive for Pleasure or Show
To Be a Harness Racer**

Written by

Cynthia Tunstall

Edited by
Toni M. Leland

Printed in U.S.A.

Published by

SMALL HORSE PRESS

a division of Equine Graphics Publishing

This book is lovingly dedicated to Nikki, my very own Miniature Horse, and my beautiful Arabian mare, Alieea. They both inspired my to put these pages together.

First Edition

Library of Congress Card Number: 95-74741
ISBN Number: 1-887932-01-1

TABLE OF CONTENT

Introduction

Miniature horses can be traced back hundreds of years, and though there are several conflicting theories about how they actually originated, one fact has been true all along. These small-engine equines delight young and old alike. Their diminutive size and sweet temperament allow absolutely anyone to enjoy training, showing, or driving a cart pulled by a Miniature Horse.

The purpose of this book is to show how you can train your own Mini for pleasure or to show. In addition, the section on conformation provides you with an outline of what to look for in a Miniature Horse, to help you make the correct decisions when shopping for a Mini or assessing horses you may already own. In the chapters that follow, you'll find some basic training instruction to get you started, including an entire chapter on teaching your Mini about horse trailers. Good sound guidance on training Minis to show in halter and conformation classes and teaching Minis to drive is covered in depth. For fans of harness racing, the section on driving has been expanded to include this new sport. Those of you who are interested in race training will appreciate the details shared by some of the top racing trainers in the country.

Even if you have no intention of showing or racing your Miniature, this book will help you train your horse, so that both of you can enjoy working as a team. The bond of trust that exists between horse and owner is a very special one and, hopefully, one that will give you hours of pleasure and a warmth that will last a lifetime.

Chapter One

Conformation
(Or, You Can't Get There From Here!)

L. Ingles

Conformation is the way a Miniature Horse is put together. All parts of the horse should flow smoothly from head to tail. Poor conformation does not necessarily mean that the horse is unsound, but it can lead to unsoundness. *"The horse is sound"* is a phrase used to describe a horse that is healthy and free of blemishes and any physical imperfections that may lessen its ability to move smoothly and easily. There should be a presence about the horse that impresses you. But most importantly, you must be sure that the animal is suitable for your goals. When considering the purchase of a Miniature Horse, your primary objective is to decide on your goals *before* purchasing the horse.

Is your Mini going to be a pet, a show horse, a pleasure driving horse, or are you interested in racing your horse? If you want a pet, then the horse's physical make-up can be less perfect than you would require for a *performance*, breeding, or racing Miniature Horse.

Should the horse be suitable for adults? Or children? If the Mini is for small children, it should be friendly and easy to handle.

Are you thinking about starting a breeding program and selling your horses? If you are starting a breeding program for show or race horses, you will want an animal that is as close to perfection as you can find. For those who want to start a breeding program specifically for racing Miniatures, athletic ability as well as good conformation are important qualities.

These are questions that should be answered *before* you buy your Miniature. Unfortunately, a lot of people don't have the answers first and, after purchasing the horse, find that it falls short of their expectations. When looking for your Miniature Horse, try to look down the road at your future plans; making these decisions before-hand will enable you to find the right Miniature the first time.

WHAT IS TYPE?

All horse breeds have certain characteristics, or *types*, which are desirable to some and not to others. Minis are no exception to this rule. There are two basic types type of Miniature Horses, and a third newer, specialty type of Miniature athlete. Most Miniature Horses are categorized into either the refined Arabian type or the heavier-bodied Quarter Horse or draft horse type. The third type—the Harnessbred—is registered with the International Miniature Trotting & Pacing Association (IMTPA), a racing registry for Minis 38 inches and under.

The Arabian type Mini has a refined body and a beautiful head. These horses have large eyes set low and wide apart, and a head that tapers from the wide forehead into a smaller-than-average *muzzle*. When viewed from the side, the head appears to be dished rather than flat. Arabian-type Minis carry their tails higher when in motion and their conformation is more graceful and delicate overall.

Note the fine muzzle and dished face on the Arabian-type Mini above. (C. Tunstall)

A stockier body characterizes the Quarter Horse-type Mini at right.

L. Ingles

The Quarter Horse or draft type Miniature is heavier in the body and has a more rounded appearance overall. Stocky and heavily-boned, characteristics of this Miniature Horse type include a broad, short head, a slightly thicker neck, and more powerful hindquarters that provide more *propulsion*. This type of Mini is well-known and popular because of its calm and even-natured disposition.

The Harnessbred Miniature Horse, the newest type in the Miniature breed, is still undergoing changes through its evolution to a smaller size. Unlike the other breed types that took years to accomplish, this specific Miniature type progressed faster for several reasons. First, it was bred from existing Miniatures that were crossed with smaller trotting horses, such as Hackney Ponies. In the first year of the breeding program, this combination has already produced foals

that mature under 36 inches. Second, trotting-type ponies have a naturally-extended trotting gait which is passed along to the Miniature and is greatly desired for racing.

This month-old Harnessbred Miniature foal shows promise for the future of Miniature Harness Racing

C. Tunstall

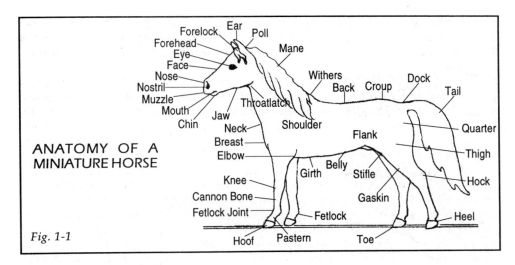

Fig. 1-1

Labels in figure: Forelock, Ear, Poll, Forehead, Mane, Eye, Face, Withers, Dock, Nose, Back, Croup, Tail, Nostril, Muzzle, Throatlatch, Mouth, Jaw, Shoulder, Quarter, Chin, Neck, Flank, Thigh, Breast, Elbow, Belly, Knee, Girth, Stifle, Hock, Cannon Bone, Gaskin, Fetlock Joint, Fetlock, Heel, Hoof, Pastern, Toe

ANATOMY OF A MINIATURE HORSE

CONFORMATION BASICS 101

When planning a breeding program, the conformation of the horse will be your first concern. The main conformation points of a horse should be assessed when looking at a prospective purchase. *(See Figure 1-1)*

The first thing to assess is that the Mini is well-balanced, small, and sound; specifically, the horse should conform to the following guidelines.

Head—Not excessively long or short, but in proportion to the body. The ears should open turned forward and be upright and alert. The mouth and teeth should show no signs of overbite or underbite; the teeth should come together evenly. The eyes should be large, bright, alert, and the same color.

Muzzle—Small, yet not too fine, with large nostrils.

Jaw—Well-defined; with wide space between the two branches of the jaw.

Neck—Well-muscled and balanced with the rest of the horse. There should be a distinct and well-defined *throat-latch*; this allows the head to flex at the poll.

Chest—Deep and full, with long ribs.

Legs—Straight and free of any physical defects.

Hooves—Round and compact, in good condition on visual examination, free of cracks, and with a small heel. For Miniature height purposes, the feet should be as short as is possible for an unshod horse.

Color—Any color and/or marking.

Hindquarters—The highest point of the hindquarters should be equal with the height of the *withers*. The tail should round off the rump of the horse and be set neither too high nor too low.

Shoulder—Long and sloping to allow the horse freedom of movement; should have a well-developed forearm.

Unacceptable conformation points can vary, depending on the registry. For registration in the "A" Division of the American Miniature Horse Registry (AMHR), horses cannot measure over 34 inches; for the "B" Division, horses must not be taller than 38 inches.

For registration in the American Miniature Horse Association (AMHA), the height must not exceed 34 inches. Other points to consider as faults are blindness, dwarfism, any unsoundness, and *cryptorchidism* in stallions.

WHY IS CONFORMATION SO IMPORTANT?

Many problems stem from Miniature Horses with poor conformation, especially in breeding stock. For example, if a Mini's lower jaw is not wide and well-defined, it can interfere with the horse's breathing during exertion. Other deformities in the set of the jaw, such as *parrot mouth* or *monkey mouth*, are considered to be unsound and are often passed on to the offspring. *(See figures 1-2 & 1-3)* These horses have a harder time chewing and digesting their food and require additional care and feeding. Miniatures of the Arabian type have wider jaws, which is considered to be a desirable quality.

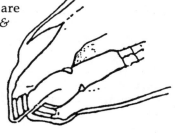

Fig. 1-2: Parrot Mouth

An overly-large head places a strain on the forehead, requiring more muscles in the neck to be used to hold the head in position; this tires the horse more easily. This is especially to be avoided if the Miniature is being considered for a harness racing horse, since you are looking for a horse with energy to spare.

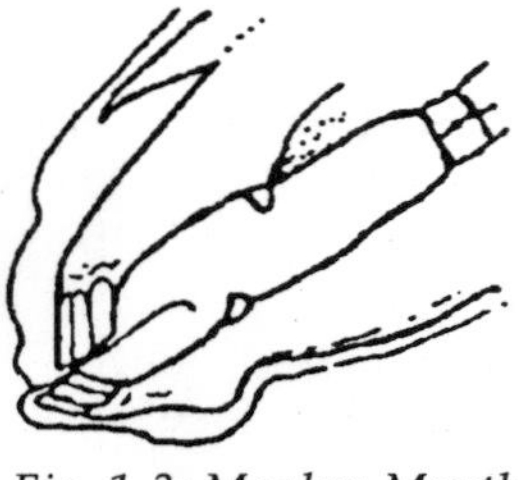

Fig. 1-3: Monkey Mouth

The way the horse holds its head depends on the shape of the neck. If not set properly, the neck can cause compression of the larynx and interfere with the horse's breathing. This conformation fault is sometimes known as "cock- throttled," because it looks similar to the way a chicken's head is set on its neck—almost in an upright position. Additionally, this horse will not bridle well or carry its head correctly. The neck should be another consideration in harness-racing Miniatures, since they need to hold their heads in the proper position to get better *impulsion* off their hindquarters.

A poorly-formed chest does not allow enough room for the heart and lungs to function properly. This is an unsuitable situation for performance horses that exert themselves. If the chest is too narrow, the legs will be too close together and restrict the horse's movements. If the chest is too wide, the horse will expend more energy performing its work.

The horse's withers should be well-defined: not too high and, in trotting-type horses, very low withers will interfere with the mobility of the shoulder. The horse's back should be short and strong. Horses with odd back conformation do not lie down as much as other horses and, as a result, their working life is shortened.[1]

A nearly horizontal *croup* is ideal for halter-type horses, although in Miniature racers, a croup with a slight slope produces faster speeds. The conformation of the croup also affects the pelvis and the connection of the hind legs and flank.

An ample slope of the shoulder is necessary for the large and powerful muscles contained in that area. Upright shoulders make the horse's gaits shorter. Elbows that are turned inward make the feet turn outward and vice versa. This puts undue strain on the *fetlock joints* and feet, and can lead to lameness in the lower legs.

The forearm should be thick, wide, long, and well-developed. In trotting horses that have high knee action, the forearm are usually short; however, if the forearm is too short, this will cause a choppy gait.

Knees should be flat and free from roundness. Small round knees cannot absorb the horse's weight when it impacts with the ground. The knee absorbs a large amount of strain and should be a primary concern when considering a Miniature Horse that will race.

One of the most common parts of the horse to develop lameness is the cannon bone. This bone should be short and strong with ample width from front to back—not so much the amount of bone, but the quality of the bone itself. A round cannon bone will not stand up to hard work.

"No foot no horse."—an old, but true expression. Bad hooves limit the usefulness of any horse, including Miniatures. The depth of the heel is of great importance because, without depth, the heel is considered to be weak and the horse will not remain sound. This can lead to *navicular* injury or *coffin bone* injury and resultant *osteitis*.

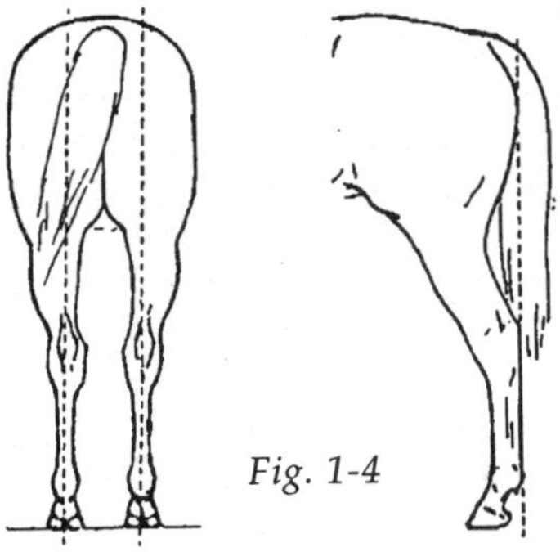

Fig. 1-4

The Miniature Horse should have well-developed hocks, which are essential for propulsion and soundness. The hock should be large, wide, and deep. Common faults to be avoided are *cow hocks* (hocks that point inward toward each other) and *bowed hocks* (hocks that turn away from each other). Hocks should be viewed from the back and the side of the horse. *(See figure 1-4)* Viewing the horse from the side, picture an imaginary line from the hip joint that falls between the heel and toe of the hoof. Viewed from the back, using the center point of the buttock, this same line should fall evenly down the center of the legs.

A Mini that has good conformation will have good movement and will be less likely to have unsoundness problems. The horse should move straight and true with no *winging* or *paddling*. Trotting-type horses should pick up their feet and cover ground without putting the feet down in the same place. This is one of the more desirable traits to look for in a potential harness-racing Miniature.

RACING CONFORMATION

While we're talking about racing Minis, there are a few specific conformation points that will help you choose a Miniature that can give you the competitive edge.

1. Large nostrils to take in larger amounts of air.
2. A long neck to add that extra inch at the finish line.
3. A fully-developed chest that is well-muscled and deep; this means more stamina.
4. Angled shoulders that provide more freedom of movement.
5. A longer back between the withers and croup.
6. Slightly higher hindquarters that slope downward toward the *dock* of the tail.
7. Legs that are the same distance, or slightly longer, from the middle of the knee to the upper forearm, and the same distance from the middle of the knee to the pastern.
8. The ability to work. Have the owner work the horse and watch for leg extension and impulsion off the hindquarters. Long legs do not always make a winning Mini racer. What does count is the horse's "heart," or desire and will to win, combined with natural athletic ability.

Good conformation is of primary importance to every horse's health, but don't discount a horse that is in poor condition if he has good conformation and is sound. A little care and the right nutrition can produce rewarding results.

No matter what you plan for your Miniature Horse, conformation plays a major role. In the show ring, not only will the horse have to be conformationally correct, but will need to have that extra *"Hey! Look At Me"* attitude that sets the horse apart from the others in the class. This is not an asset that you can see, but it is as much a part of the horse as its body. It is the horse's personality—an air of self-confidence and a noble, yet knowing look in the eye—that radiates the spirit within the Miniature Horse.

1 Hayes, Capt. M. Horace, FRCV's. <u>Veterinary Notes For Horse Owners</u>. Rossdale, Peter D., PhD, Ed., Simon & Schuster, 17th Revised Edition.

Chapter Two

Basic Training
(Or, Boot Camp for Babies)

ACCEPTING A HALTER & LEARNING TO LEAD

Horse trainers everywhere will agree on one thing when it comes to training a horse: the earlier you handle them, the better companions they will be as adult horses. If you listen and watch, horses can tell you what they like and don't like. For example, if you are holding your Miniature and he starts pushing you with his head, it's a safe bet to assume that he is annoyed and would prefer to be left alone. It is a wise horse trainer who notices this and, instead of forcing the issue, distracts the horse. By changing the lesson area or giving the horse a break, you will be able to take his mind off what he doesn't want to do.

P. Perry

Routine also keeps Miniatures happy, since horses learn by repetition. They know when it is close to feeding time. If you're not there when they think you should be, they'll chew on the fence or find some other way to entertain themselves until you arrive! Pay attention to how your Mini reacts—does he seem concerned or does he look like he's bored? Noticing and watching your Mini will teach you to anticipate possible behavior problems before they arise.

One of the biggest accomplishments in training your Mini will be getting to know his likes and dislikes. Pay attention to how your horse reacts to different situations. For instance, when you pet or scratch your Mini, watch his nose. A sure sign that the horse likes what you're doing or that you've hit that special itchy place is when his nose "scrunches" up. That's a happy horse!

BABES IN THE BARN

Foals should be trained to accept a halter within the first few days of life. The importance of handling new foals can't be over-emphasized. This imprint method involves repeatedly handling a foal soon after birth to encourage the horse's acceptance of the handler as its master. A horse that is handled from birth, whether it's a Miniature or a large one, will come to accept your attentions as a pleasant experience and look forward to having you around. In addition, you will have established a "pecking order" where *you* are in charge.

L. Ingles

To accustom your Mini foal to the halter, you should start by touching him all over, concentrating your attention around his head and ears. Once he accepts handling of his head and ears, it should not concern him when the halter is placed on his head.

An important note: during the imprint process, never interfere when the foal wants to go to his mother; the foal needs to be able to go to his mother for security and to nurse. When working around mare and foal, always step back if either of the horses wants access to the other. Failure to do so will cause the mare to be over-protective and view you as a threat to her baby. Instead, you want both the mare and the foal to think of you as part of their family and someone to be trusted

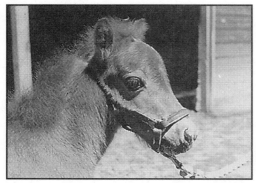
L. Ingles

The first time you put the halter on your Mini, leave it on for a short period of time—about 15-30 minutes on the first day. Be sure to stay close by—you will not want this to be a bad experience. Do not attempt to lead the foal at this point. Horses need to become comfortable with one thing before you move on to another. Increase the amount of time your foal wears the halter during the first week until you feel he has settled in and accepted it.

All horses can benefit from imprint training, even older horses or those who have been abused or neglected by previous owners. In these cases, it is up to you to undo the bad habits that the Mini has acquired. The best place to start is at Ground Zero. Even the simple act of putting on a halter might have been a past bad experience for your Mini, but a little time, love, and attention will go a long way toward repairing a sour horse.

MAKING USE OF YOUR HALTER TRAINING TIME

Since the halter is a new experience for your Mini, necessitating some supervision, you can take advantage of this time by getting the horse accustomed to having its feet handled. The first time you work with the feet, confine the session to a stall where your Mini feels safe. When asking the Mini to lift a hoof for the first time, keep in mind that he is like a small child learning to walk: awkward and clumsy.

Make sure the horse is standing squarely and is well-balanced. Run your hand down his leg, applying slight pressure to the back of the cannon bone where the flexor tendon is located. This technique will usually make the horse lift its foot. Once the horse picks the foot up, grasp the hoof in your hand.Praise him with a few pats and soft words, then put the hoof down. Do the same thing with the other three feet, but don't attempt to do anything more at this point. *(See figures 2-1 & 2-2)*

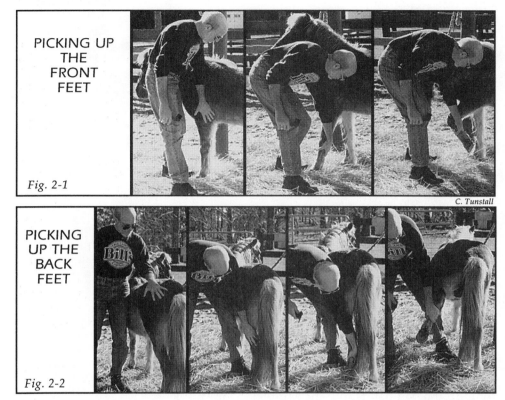

PICKING UP THE FRONT FEET

Fig. 2-1

C. Tunstall

PICKING UP THE BACK FEET

Fig. 2-2

Your Mini will gradually understand that when you do this, he is supposed to lift his foot. Sometimes horses learn this lesson so well that, the minute you put one foot down, they are picking up the next one for you!

At this stage, your Miniature should feel comfortable wearing a halter and having his feet handled. Now it is time to attach a lead rope to the halter.

FOLLOW THE LEADER

All horses like to be around other horses. They will follow the example of another horse more quickly than they will respond to you. For instance, many horses are naturally distrustful of water and will always walk around it, if given the option. But there will be times when your Miniature will have to walk through water. If you have another Mini that is accustomed to walking through water, lead him through first and the other one will follow.

The quickest way to teach a Miniature foal to lead is to use his mother as an example. If your stall is large enough, this is the best place to start the first lesson; otherwise, choose another confined area so that the foal will always be close by. Halter both horses and lead the mare around, either along a fence or in a small circle, and the foal will follow his mother naturally. He will remember this as a good experience and, if Mom does it—it must be okay! When

Using another horse helps teach your Mini to lead. (C. Tunstall)

possible, take advantage of using another well-trained horse to help teach a youngster and even older Miniatures can be trained using this technique. Using one Miniature to train another will make your lessons go more quickly and teach the horse to trust you, which will be very valuable later on.

Always train your Miniature in a restricted area. If the horse bolts, you'll be able to catch him more easily. Never physically fight with your horse. Even though they are little, do not under-estimate the strength of these tiny horses. Once a battle between you and your Miniature takes place, it will take twice as long to undo the damage. Furthermore, fighting teaches the horse bad habits such as rearing, kicking, and tossing its head around. Use your brain, not your muscles, to make your Mini understand your requests.

The foal's first solo lead-line lesson can be conducted in the pasture with the mother close by. Stand in front of your Miniature and ask him to walk while you pull on the rope. Then release the pressure on the rope. The use of continuous

(C. Lekstrom)

pressure will cause the horse to resist. Instead, pull with a firm, yet gentle "pull-and-release" until the horse takes one step toward you. Once he takes that first step, reward him with pats and praise. If he starts pulling backwards the first few times he is asked to *"walk,"* don't fight it—give him some slack and go with the horse. Once he stops, let him get comfortable, eat some grass, or go to his mother for a few minutes. Then start over.

For a resistant horse that won't move forward, one trick is to turn his head in a direction other than straight ahead. Turning the head does two things: first, he's uncomfortable with his head one way and his body the other, and second, it puts him slightly off balance. The result should be that he takes a step to make himself more comfortable. Once he takes the first step, you keep walking and the horse will follow. Eventually, he will learn to move forward on command or with just a slight tug on the lead line.

Lessons should be short and productive. The length of the lesson is not important; five good minutes are better than 20 minutes with a horse that is uncooperative. Foals have a limited attention span and become bored quickly, but with limited daily practice, your Mini foal will produce rewarding results.

HALTER SENSE!

It is unwise to leave any haltered horse unattended. It is a wise trainer who only puts a halter on a horse if there is a need to do so, instead of leaving it on the horse all the time. Horses are naturally curious and, left to their own devices, they find plenty of ways to get into trouble. Leaving a halter on a horse (especially a nylon halter that will not break) just invites trouble. Your Mini could get caught on something or tangled up in fencing and very possibly be injured in the process. You can avoid any halter-related mishaps by limiting the use of a halter to those times when you are working with your horse.

"WHOA!" THE MOST USED WORD IN TRAINING

At six months of age, your foal will mature into a weanling and you can start working on "walk" and "trot" commands. By this time, you should be able to walk alongside your Miniature at his shoulder. Now, ask him to *"Walk,"* and you take a step. Then ask him to *"Whoa"* and you stop walking. Repeat this exercise several times in each session. Each time the horse steps forward and then stops on your command, praise him. The horse should respond to your voice and then stand quietly for progressively longer periods of time. Just remember that the horse is still a youngster and has a limited attention span.

THE CROP

Before progressing to the next level of ground work, your Miniature should be introduced to yet another new training aid, the crop. Different trainers prefer different crops, but for teaching the young horse, a short crop of any type will work. Show him the crop and let him smell it. (One helpful tip is to stick the end of the crop into some feed so that the horse likes the way it smells!)

The crop is a training tool and is not to be used as a means of punishment. If the horse fears the crop, he will not respond to your request and this can result in behavior problems. Use the crop only to encourage the horse to move on command; usually, just showing it to him will do the trick. If not, a slight tap on the hindquarters will always work. Your Miniature should respect this aid, but never be fearful.

TEACHING YOUR MINI TO TROT ON COMMAND

The next lesson in flat work is teaching the horse to trot on command. Start out by walking beside him, then pick up speed, and tell him to *"Trot."* If he needs a little encouragement, try clucking and, if that doesn't work, give him a slight tap with the crop. Some horses get very excited when you're running alongside them and can get going a little faster than you can manage. This is where all your "walk" and "whoa" commands suddenly become very useful. If your Miniature starts to get out of control, jerk downward on the lead-line a couple of times to get his attention, and loudly say "Whoa"! The stern tone of voice and volume of the command are very important. The horse must understand that you are the one in control. Once he comes back to a walk or stops, pat him and praise him for responding to your commands.

BACKING UP

Once your Miniature is walking and trotting on command, it's time to teach him to back up. For this lesson, place the horse beside a fence, barn, or other building. While applying backward pressure on the lead rope and giving a little push on the chest, say "Back." The reason for using the fence or building is to encourage the horse to back up in a straight line. If the horse takes only one step, offer praise and a little reward.

Your Miniature should back up four to five steps as the lessons progress. Always ask him to walk forward after backing. Backing up on his own, without your command, can become an annoying bad habit. By asking the horse to go forward after backing up, you will eliminate the possibility of the horse using this maneuver at will.

Walking, trotting, or backing the horse along a fence or wall will encourage him to move in a straight line. Be sure you work both sides of your horse in all training sessions. If the horse's right side is on the fence line, the next pass should be with his left side on the fence line. The purpose of exercising both sides of the horse is to develop the muscles equally. When you progress to lunging your horse, neglecting to work the horse on both sides can result in leg strain and resultant uneven gaits.

By the age of one year, your Mini should know and respond to the voice commands of "walk," "trot," "back," and "whoa." You now can move on to the application of exercise for conditioning your horse.

LUNGE FORWARD FOR EXERCISE

Exercise is instrumental in keeping your Mini in good physical conditioning. Lunging is an exercise regime that allows the horse's training to progress at a rate that will permit his legs to finish developing fully. Lunging will also accustom your Mini to working on his own.

The lunge line is a very useful tool because, by working the horse in a circular pattern, the exercise strengthens the muscles. Some trainers use round pens, which are specially built rings about 20 feet in diameter. In a round pen, you don't need to use a lunge line (although it's advisable at first); instead, you can

Lunging your Mini provides both exercise and discipline. (T. Leland)

stand in the center and give the horse the commands to "walk," "trot," and "whoa."

Lunge lines are simply a longer version of a lead rope (approximately 15-20 feet in length). Commercial lunge lines are made of 1-inch wide nylon and have a chain with a clip on one end with which to attach to the halter. Newer versions come equipped with a flat, round disk on the handler's end that keeps the line from being pulled out of your hand.

You can, however, make a lunge line out of rope, preferably a sturdy cotton-type that will not burn your hands should it pull free. (A tip: It is advisable to wear gloves while lunging a horse.) Simply place a clip on one end and a large knot on the other, and you have a lunge line!

To start your Mini with basic lunging, attach the lunge line by running the chain through the near-side ring of the halter, passing it under the chin, and clipping it to the halter ring on the opposite side. *(See figure 2-3)* The chain serves a purpose: to get the horse's attention and to help move his head in the direction you want him to follow, which is in a circle, for our purposes here. Don't forget to have your crop along; you will need it as an aid during these lessons.

Start out as usual with your walk and trot lessons. Horses learn faster if you start them off with a familiar lesson. Take your Mini out to the pasture or any open area. Walk him around for a few minutes and then stand still. Using the crop to encourage him, ask the horse to walk around you in a small circle, while you stand stationary. The horse is bound to be confused the first few times and

Fig. 2-3

will probably stop and look at you with that *"I don't understand"* look. For the first lesson in lunging, it is a good idea to have a helper who can hold onto the halter and walk the horse to show him what he is being asked to do.

When you ask the horse to *"Walk,"* the helper should take a step and walk the horse around you in a circle. To make the horse stop walking, say *"Whoa."* The helper should stop walking at the same time. Reverse the process in the opposite direction until the horse is used to you standing still while he moves around in a circle. This lesson should not be more than 10 to 20 minutes. This process may have to be repeated several times with a helper to get the horse accustomed to working at a distance from you.

If you do this every day, by the end of the first week, the horse should understand and be able to progress without the aid of the helper. Only ask your

Mini to "walk" and "whoa" during these first few solo lessons. After he is walking quietly around you, it is time to ask him to trot. During the first rotting lesson on the lunge line, ask your horse to *"Walk,"* then cluck to him, and then, in a strong voice, ask him to *"Trot."* If he needs a little encouragement, show him the crop. Remember to work the horse in both directions so that he gets equal exercise on both sides of his body.

Gradually build up the length of time you require him to walk and trot slowly. You do not want to tire the horse or put undue stress on his legs. The length of each of these training sessions should be no more than 20 minutes.

During these early lessons, the circles should be small, gradually building to larger circles. Whenever the horse has performed a gait gaits to your satisfaction, praise him with your voice. Miniatures learn quickly and will respond to your voice and praise. Some horses will take advantage of the situation and try to walk over to you. Make it a point to keep the horse away from you; discourage him from moving out of his circle by holding out the crop. Instead, once you ask him to *"Whoa,"* immediately walk over to him and give him pats and praise.

In later chapters, your sessions will incorporate some more gaits and lunging exercises designed to fit specific tasks that you will ask of your Miniature Horse.

TEACHING YOUR MINIATURE TO TIE

Once you have mastered "starting" and "stopping" your horse and making him go 'round in circles, the next training phase is to introduce your Miniature to being tied.

There are several ways to tie your horse. One of the safest ways is by the use of cross-ties. This system consists of two poles, standing approximately 5 to 6 feet apart and 5 to 6 feet high, buried into the ground deep enough to be immobile. *(See Figure 2-4)* The poles should have large metal "O" rings inserted into them; these should be placed high enough so that the horse can lift his head about a foot, but not so high as to allow the horse to rear-up. The "O" rings enable you to use quick-release clips; should the horse become frightened, just one tug on the clip will release the tie. If you don't have cross-ties, a tree will work just as well.

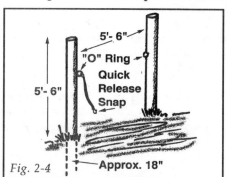

5'- 6"

"O" Ring

Quick Release Snap

5'- 6"

Fig. 2-4   Approx. 18"

During this first lesson, do not attach the clips or tie the rope! Instead, just hold your end and watch the horse's response. He'll figure out very shortly that he is caught and can't move more than a few steps. If he looks even slightly concerned, talk to him softly while standing next to him and, for reassurance, give him a couple of pats. If you need to distract him, using a little grain or a few pieces of carrot is all right. If there is any indication that the horse is going to rear, bolt, or anything else inappropriate, give him some slack in the rope. In the worst case, release the horse BEFORE he makes the attempt.

Perseverance is the key! Keep at it until your Mini understands that this will not hurt him and he accepts being tied. Progress slowly and always stop on a good note. If the horse misbehaves during a lesson, go back to something that he did well and have him do that exercise properly. Again, avoid any confrontations with your Miniature during these training sessions.

GROOMING

Once your Miniature is accustomed to being tied, it will be easier for you to groom him. Most horses enjoy being brushed and usually won't get too concerned while you're grooming. Grooming feels good and stimulates the skin. This is also your chance to check for any small cuts, scratches, bruises, or heat or swelling in the legs. Having this regular inspection time can really help in spotting a problem before it gets serious, thus saving you costly veterinary visits.

Cleaning the hooves ensures that nothing is wedged between the frog and the sole of the hoof. Regular cleaning prevents bacteria from building up. Failure to clean the hooves regularly can lead to *thrush*, a degenerative condition of the frog. Unchecked, thrush can cause lameness.

If you're using cross-ties, be sure to use those quick-release clips. If using a plain rope, be sure you can tie a quick-release or slip knot. *(See figure 2-5)* Always be ready! Even the calmest horses can suddenly react, catching the handler off guard.

Keeping feet clean is an important part of your Mini's daily routine. (C. Tunstall)

At the completion of this phase of training, you should be able to pick up and clean your Miniature's hooves, and brush and comb him while he is tied.

CLIPPING—A SCARY EXPERIENCE!

Why should you clip your Mini? Miniatures tend to be woolly and sometimes do not shed their winter coats fast enough as warm weather approaches. Having a left-over winter coat in 90-degree weather is uncomfortable and definitely not desirable if you plan to show your Miniature.

Part of the care of your Miniature Horse includes clipping the haircoat. Clipping

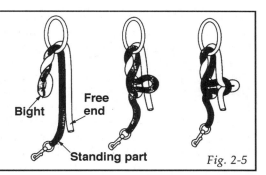

The Quick Release Knot

1— Pass a u-loop through the ring. Twist tightly 2 or 3 turns.
2— Pass a u-loop of the standing part through the first loop.
3— Pass a u-loop of the free end through the second u-loop

Bight   Free end

Standing part   *Fig. 2-5*

horses is a necessity for their comfort and to make them look their best for the show ring. Some horses take clipping in stride; others never get used to it. But all horses can be taught to tolerate the process.

Tie the horse and try to have a helper standing by during the horse's first few experiences with the clippers. Make sure that the electric cord is out of the way to eliminate the possibility of the horse becoming entangled if he gets nervous.

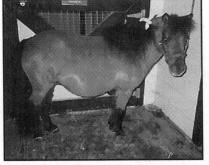

Under all that hair was a pregnant Mini!
(C. Lekstrom)

Turn the clippers on and let your Mini hear the noise. Since the noise is sudden and unexpected, it may frighten him the first few times. Be prepared! Hold the clippers far enough away so that he does not feel threatened. With the clippers running, gradually move closer to the horse, talking to him all the while.

At this point, if your Miniature seems unconcerned, place the clippers against his shoulder (with the blades turned *away* from the horse). This will help accustom him to the vibration. Talk reassuringly and pat him softly with your free hand. Encourage his good behavior. Now, slowly move the clippers around on his shoulder and let him settle down.

Move the clippers slowly up his neck toward the mane, where you will need to clip the bridle path. The bridle path is located where the halter or bridle strap runs across the top of the horse's head. Different breeds have a bridle path cut in different lengths. With Mini's, the basic rule is that, if you could lay his ears flat against his neck, that would be the length to cut the bridle path. This is approximately four inches from the poll back toward the mane. This area is usually easiest to do. The ears, on the other hand, seem to always be a point of contention with a horse that is being clipped. Since it is disagreeable to the horse, clipping the ears should be the last lesson.

You may or may not be able to actually clip your Mini in this first session. The thing to remember is to end on a good note, even if all you accomplish is getting him to accept having the clippers placed on his body.

When your Miniature seems to be taking the clipper noise and vibration in stride, try clipping either the bridle path or the muzzle. Some horses try to eat the clippers or wrinkle up their nose because the vibration tickles, but as long as they are not afraid, keep on clipping. Remember that this area is sensitive and tender, especially around the nostrils and the lips. Keep the clippers well-oiled; this helps lessen the noise and ensures they are running smoothly. Always check the blades for broken teeth that could cut or pinch the horse's skin.

For Miniatures you will need two types of clippers for grooming: a lighter set for the mane, muzzle, and ears and another heavy-duty set for the body. Some owners prefer using a round-edge scissors for the face area, but this is very time-consuming and a young horse will become impatient. Electric clippers are faster and do a better job.

THE TWITCH—A LOVE-HATE TOOL

You may have to use a twitch to distract your Mini the first time you clip his ears. A twitch is a tool used to distract the horse by applying pressure to the nose. It is best to introduce your horse to the twitch early, in preparation for the times when the veterinarian needs to perform necessary exams or routine treatments (such as tube worming).

Most horse lovers hate the twitch, but many times find it nec- essary and useful.

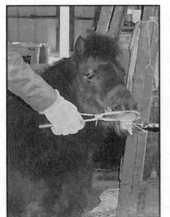

Using a "tubing twitch" for routine veterinary care. (L. Ingles)

There are many types of twitches, but the most humane type is the one used by veterinarians. It consists of a length of wooden broom handle with a hole drilled through one end. A 14-inch length of soft cotton rope (about 1/4 to 1/2 inch in diameter) is doubled over and the free ends are slipped through the hole and knotted on the other side. (See fig. 2-6)

To use the twitch place your hand through the loop of cotton, grasp the horse's nose, and place the rope over and behind the hand holding the nose. Once the rope is in place, use your free hand to twist the wooden handle until the rope tightens up enough to stay in place without slipping off. At this point, you can let go of the nose with your hand. Note—the more

14" rope

knot end
of rope

approx. 12"

Fig. 2-6

you twist the handle, the more pressure is applied to the horse's nose. It is **highly** recommended that you start out using the least amount of pressure possible, and only slightly increasing it as needed to distract your Mini.

Always remember that the twitch is a tool used to distract your horse, not a means of punishment. It is an aid to allow you or your veterinarian to perform procedures that your Mini would not stand still enough to have done.

Chapter Three

Trailer Training
(Or, You Gotta Start Somewhere!)

If there is any chance, now or later, that you'll want to take your Miniature anywhere, whether it's to a show, racing event, or the vet, one thing is a given: the horse must learn to load into a horse trailer. Even in breeding programs, horses travel to other farms or to new owners. Teaching your horse to load is a part of basic training that can eliminate the risk of injury to your Mini or yourself.

There are two types of horse trailers: trailers with ramps and "step-up" trailers. Every horse owner has a preference; some like ramps, some don't. It's a very individual choice. Here are some examples of the differences between the two types of trailers.

STEP-UP TRAILER

A Mini trailer with a ramp entrance. (C.Tunstall)

Ramp-type trailers allow the horse to walk up the inclined ramp and into the trailer. Step-up trailers require the horse to put his foot up higher (most are 8 to 12 inches off the ground); this can put the horse off balance. Actual use of both trailer types by this author, plus conversations with various trainers, provides the "bad news" on the two types. In ramp trailers, the horse can slip off the ramp. In step-up trailers, if the horse refuses to enter, then backs up quickly, the horse's hind legs can slip underneath the edge of the trailer. This author's personal experience with horses has shown that particularly spooky horses tend to jump into trailers that don't have ramps. This is a less-controlled entry and is, therefore, more risky.

Horses are naturally wary of strange things and, to them, the horse trailer is the "bogeyman." It is a good idea to place the horse trailer where the horse can see it for a few days before beginning the loading lessons. This will allow your horse to become accustomed to its presence.

If the trailer has a ramp, put the ramp down; otherwise, open the rear loading doors. If your trailer has windows or a front escape door, make sure that they are open. Since all horses are distrustful of dark places, the brighter the trailer is, the more quickly the horse will go inside.

THAT FIRST STEP

You can teach your Miniature Horse to load in about one week, if you follow this simple training technique. Many horse owners use hay and grain to teach their horses to load, but with this technique, your Mini will load without coaxing and be more relaxed about the trailer.

Give your Mini plenty of time to get acquainted with the horse trailer. (C.Tunstall)

Attach a lead rope to your Mini's halter and walk him up to the trailer. Let him sniff all around it. Then, walking alongside the horse's shoulder, ask him to follow you up to the ramp or to the back of the trailer. Let him get a good look inside. Talk softly, pat him, and say *"Good"* for even the slightest progress. Next, ask the horse to put one foot on the trailer ramp or floor. If he puts his foot up, praise him again, and do not force him to do anything more. Let him move back to his "safe zone"— about 6 to 10 feet away from the trailer.

Do not rush your Mini! Let him eat some grass, wait about two minutes, and ask him to put his foot on the trailer again. Encourage him and always praise his good behavior. That is the end of the first lesson!

The next day, repeat the process and try to get him to keep his foot in the trailer or on the ramp for about 5 or 10 seconds. Say *"Whoa"* and *"Good,"* encouraging him to stand quietly. Let him retreat again to his safe zone and eat grass.

Both feet on the ramp! (C.Tunstall)

Repeat the process, asking him again to put his foot on the ramp or in the trailer. If he's agreeable, ask for the second foot. If you get both front feet in the trailer for even one second, you've made progress!

Some horses try to avoid the trailer by moving off in a sideways direction. Or, in the case of a trailer with a ramp, the horse might try to walk off the ramp. This is where your previous lessons with the crop and lunge whip come in handy.

AIDS AND ENCOURAGEMENT

As your Mini is moving toward the open trailer, take up a position next to the opening. Place the crop in your free hand and hold it out in a direct line with the trailer to discourage him from moving off in that direction. If you've used the crop in flat work, your Mini already respects the crop and the most you will have to do is touch him lightly to encourage him to move straight forward.

Practice loading the horse *every day* for 15 to 20 minutes, asking him to stand with his front feet in the trailer for increasingly longer periods of time. Eventually, you will work up to having all four feet either on the ramp or up the step. Once the horse stands quietly with all four feet in the trailer for 2 to 3 minutes, he is ready to load all the way into the trailer. These practice sessions will have prepared him for all the noise and movements that are associated with the trailer.

The first time you ask the horse to walk all the way into the trailer, don't be too concerned if he wants to immediately back out. Instead, let him know, that it is all right. If possible, before he makes the choice himself, say *"Back up,"* while gently pushing him backward. Be sure to help him with your voice, saying *"Easy,"* so he doesn't want to rush out of the trailer. By the end of the first week using this technique, you will be amazed at the progress your Mini has made.

During the second week of trailer lessons, practice tying your horse at the front, inside the trailer. Be sure to stay with him so that you can release him if he becomes frightened. Again, just a few seconds—long enough that your Miniature knows he is tied—is all that is required. Once he accepts being tied in the trailer, you're ready to close it up.

Have a helper on hand to shut the doors of the trailer. Leave all windows open. Be sure you've placed some hay in the haybag or rack; this will give your Mini something to do once the doors are shut.

After the doors are shut and he is standing in the trailer, reward him with a special treat like carrots or a little grain. This first period of time spent with the doors shut should be very limited—only a minute or two. Now open the doors and let him leave the trailer. Over the next few days, or however long it takes, leave the horse inside the trailer for increasingly longer periods of time. When you are sure that your Mini is comfortable with the whole idea, you can step outside the trailer and observe him through the windows to make sure that he is not nervous without you right there beside him. Keep on with the sessions daily until your Mini is perfectly happy to stand inside the trailer and munch hay, whether you are there or not.

From this point on, your horse will not fear the trailer and will usually load almost instantly.

Chapter Four

Training Your Miniature To Show at Halter
(Or, How Do I Keep His Ears Up?)

(C. Tunstall)

You've finally decided to take a crack at showing your Mini yourself. You can hardly wait! But first, you'll need to make sure your horse is well-disciplined and ready to embark on his show career. You've completed the basic training and now your Mini is ready for some advanced work.

STANDING STILL ON COMMAND

First, you will need to teach your Miniature how to stand correctly in the show ring. How he stands and behaves will determine his placement in the class. To teach him to stand squarely or "square-up," say *"Whoa,"* and using the toe of your shoe, nudge each of his hooves (either in front or behind) until he is standing evenly on both front and back feet. Sometimes you'll have to physically pick up his feet and put them into place. Be sure to praise him when he gets it right. You will find that during halter classes, some trainers and owners pick up the feet and move them into position. If you have schooled your horse correctly, he will automatically assume the correct stance and this will make a favorable impression on the judge.

Miniature Horses show to their best advantage when the front legs are just slightly in front of the chest, as opposed to a straight line from the chest down to the feet. All breed registries have different rules and allow different stances during halter classes. As an example, Quarter Horses are "set up" squarely— both front and back feet evenly under them—to show off their hind-ends (an important conformation point in this breed). The American Saddlebred shows to their best advantage by standing stretched—back legs well behind the hind-end and front legs well forward of the chest. And Arabian Horses are allowed to stretch out one hind leg and keep the front legs even with the chest; this shows off their characteristically level top line and flat croup to the fullest.

Miniature Horses are basically allowed to set up like Arabians, within the limits set by the Miniature registries. To get a better understanding of the acceptable stance in Miniature halter classes, picture a box around your horse, as viewed from the side. *(See Figure 4-1)* The sides of this imaginary box start from where the Mini's neck connects with his chest and ends at the dock of his tail. The top and bottom of this imaginary box should be from a few inches above the Mini's

YES

NO

Fig. 4-1 **Illustrations courtesy of The American Miniature Horse Association, Alvarado, Texas; reproduced from *Official Rulebook of the AMHA, 1996*.**

withers to his feet. The front legs can stretch to the edge of the box, but only one of the hind legs can be slightly outside of this frame. (The horse can have one hind leg slightly back, to show off the croup to its best advantage.) The front feet should be set together, and slightly forward, within the square. The head and neck should be at an angle that flows smoothly from withers to poll and down to the muzzle. If the muzzle of the horse is held too high or straight out, points will be deducted. The overall appearance, when looking at the horse from the side, is one of a horse with graceful flowing lines, standing at ease.

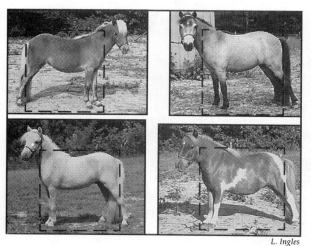

Of course, beauty is in the eye of the beholder, so keep this in mind when showing your pride and joy during a halter class. Even judges have their preferences and prejudices about breeding

From the photos at left, can you pick out which horse is standing correctly?

L. Ingles

Answer: the one in the lower left box.

and what makes a pretty Miniature Horse. Trainers and owners alike tend to categorize judges into two basic preference groups: Quarter Horse judges and Arabian judges. It is best to know before-hand which of the two types you are dealing with and set up the horse accordingly for your best chances in the class.

Teaching your Mini the proper stance will definitely take a little time, but once he has learned it, your Mini will "set-up" on his own on command.

WHERE'S THAT SWAN NECK?

Once you have trained him to stand correctly, you will want to teach him to stretch out his neck, with his ears pricked forward, while not moving from his stance. Use a little feed or anything else that will get the horse's attention, without frightening him. Stand in front of your Mini and hold out your hand, with some grain to get his attention. Using slight pressure on the lead line, encourage him to stretch his neck. If he moves his feet, say *"Whoa!"* and start over. Once he reaches out with his neck, without moving his feet, give him a nibble of the grain and lots of praise as a reward.

Have someone on hand who can stand back and view the horse to see if he is in the best position possible. The horse should look relaxed, yet interested and alert. Above all, he must stand quietly for the judge. A well-placed horse that stands quietly will stand out from the rest of the horses in the class.

Getting your Miniature to stand correctly for the judging takes practice and patience. (C. Tunstall)

KEEP THOSE EARS UP!

There is no easy way to teach a horse to look alert, keep its ears forward, or stretch its neck. Instead, it takes daily repetition. When practicing at home, use anything you can think of that will interest your horse. Try a handful of dry leaves, crunched up as you hold it out to the horse, a rag that you can shake, a metal cup filled with paper clips, or anything else that makes noise. These will interest your Mini for only a short time, so you will have to vary what you use to capture his attention. Some horses will always have a laid-back posture and attitude and will not keep their ears forward for very long, no matter what you do. If this is the case for you, then you will have to concentrate on enhancing the other good points of your Mini so that the horse will show well, even with relaxed ears.

When you find an attention-getter that works really well, save it for show time. (Be sure that anything you use in the ring is not distracting, such as plastic bags, balloons, etc. Items such as these will not be allowed by show officials.) During a halter class at a show, using a few pieces of grain or carrots held out in your hand will usually encourage your Miniature to stretch. One thing you must not allow him to do is move his feet during this stretching process. If he looks as if he is going to take a step, say *"Whoa."* Practice makes perfect on this one!

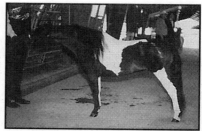

Make sure your Mini doesn't move out of his stance when stretching. (T.Leland)

IN THE RING

While you are showing your Miniature Horse, the judges will be looking at the overall impression of your horse and will judge him on conformation appropriate to the horse's sex. If your Mini is a male, he should look masculine; a mare or a filly should look feminine. Judges will also consider straight legs, a well-muscled body, a head that is in proportion to the length of neck and body, and the degree of alertness. A well-groomed and conditioned horse has an extra advantage, as well. Read and re-read your rule book to make sure you understand what is required of a halter horse, both conformationally and training-wise.

During a halter class, you will be asked to move your horse off at a walk and a trot, both individually and then with the rest of the class, so that the judge can view everyone at once. To practice at home for halter classes, begin by asking your Miniature to take up the proper stance and stretch his neck. Then ask him to go into a trot on command. Be sure you are keeping pace with your horse at his shoulder; never get ahead of or in front of the horse. The quicker your Mini responds to your commands, the better his chances will be to win the class. When asked to "Whoa," he should respond immediately. Any misbehavior such as rearing, kicking, head-tossing, or refusing to move will count against you and your horse in any class.

Your Miniature will be judged on conformation, quality, presence, "way of going," and type. With the horse on a loose lead, you will enter the ring at a walk and proceed in a counter-clockwise direction. You will walk along the rail or enclosure until you reach a marked designated area about 20 to 30 feet from the ingate. Once you and your horse have reached the location where the judges are standing, you will ask your Mini to trot by the judges and then line up with the other horses, head to tail along the rail. While in the line-up, you will set up your horse and ask him to stretch his neck. (You can use grain, pieces of carrots or other favorite treats to encourage him. Crops, whips or other such devices are not allowed in the halter classes at either AMHA- or AMHR-approved events.)

When it is your turn to show, you will walk to the judges and then trot back to the end of the line-up. Keep in mind that you should still be showing off your Mini in the line-up while the others are going by the judge. The judges notice

Train Your Own Mini

everything! If a judge likes your Miniature, he or she will be giving it second looks when you least expect it. Always be showing your horse to the best of your ability. Once all the entries have had their turn, the judges will make a decision.

(A note here: if, during the judging of AMHA or AMHR halter classes, the judge picks two horses that equally meet all of the judging criteria, the judge **must** award the blue ribbon to the smaller Miniature. However, a smaller horse can never be placed over a larger horse that has better conformation.)

Waiting for the decision. (T. Leland)

Practice this show-ring routine at home to get your Mini accustomed to working this way. The more polished the horse is in the ring, the better the odds are of taking home a blue ribbon. Work especially on the trot; the higher the action and the more brilliantly your Miniature moves, the better chance you'll have to catch the judge's eye. Your horse should be obedient and look like he's having fun and enjoying the class.

DETAILS! DETAILS! DETAILS!

Show halters can make a difference. When showing in halter classes, you have the opportunity to optimize your horse's best features or play down the poor ones. The most important detail when choosing show halters is to make sure that the halter you choose fits your horse's head.

The manner in which you place the noseband of the halter can make a Miniature's head look longer or shorter. If you have a Mini with a slightly longer face than

Proper fit of your show halter is very important. (L. Ingles)

is desirable, you'll want to place the halter so that it makes the face appear shorter. Usually, Quarter Horse-type Miniatures are shown in Western-style leather halters. Arabian-type Miniatures are shown in small, delicate, rolled-leather or cable halters that are not much bigger around than a piece of spaghetti.

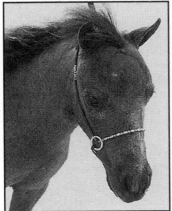

A fine cable show halter shows off delicate features (C. Tunstall)

Rule of thumb: if your horse has a plain head, then use a flashy halter. On the other hand, if the head is your horse's best asset, use a very plain, dainty halter that will not detract from the facial contours and features.

Chapter Five

Getting Ready To Drive
(Or, Bits, Bridles, and Bogeymen)

Training your Mini horse to accept new devices such as bits bridles, and harness will take some time and patience. These things should be introduced with caution, allowing your Miniature time to adjust to each new element before moving on to the next item. This chapter will give you tips and pointers on the proper use of your driving equipment and how to train your horse to drive.

It is advisable to wait until the age of two years to start training your Mini to drive. Horses are creatures of habit and learn

Driving your Mini can be one of Life's greatest pleasures! (C.Lekstrom)

easily by repetition. Once your horse becomes familiar with one piece of equipment, you can progress on to the next piece. If you move at the horse's pace, you will find him a willing and eager companion.

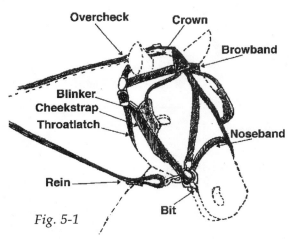

Fig. 5-1

During this training stage, you will be working with a bridle, bit and some parts of the harness. Your Miniature has already been trained to the halter, so it should not be much of an adjustment to move on to the bridle. Make sure that this is a good experience! Put just the bridle headstall on the horse (no reins). Check the length of the cheek straps and adjust, if necessary. *(See figure 5-1)* Check to see that the noseband, browband, and throatlatch

pieces are secure, but not too snug. When you have made any needed adjustments, remove the bridle from the horse. After making sure the bridle fits properly at all points, the next step is to acquaint your Miniature to the bit. Your Mini will take a little longer to become accustomed to the bit, but there are some techniques and old tricks given here that will help smooth your way.

The first bit that you will use is a fat rubber snaffle. *(See figure 5-2)* Rubber snaffles are the mildest bits available and are used for training young horses to accept the bit. This type of snaffle is soft and chewy and accustoms the horse to having something in his mouth. (The first thing your Mini will probably do is give it a good chewing!) After attaching the bit to the bridle (still with no reins), the next step will be putting the bridle back on the horse.

To place the bit into the horse's mouth, stand alongside the head on his left side. Grasp the bridle by the top (browband or head band) with your right hand, hold it in front of the Mini's face, with the bit in your left hand. Angle the top of the bridle slightly toward his ears. Insert your finger midway along the side of the horse's mouth to encourage him to open his jaw. This usually works because horses do not like the taste of our fingers. If needed, you can tickle the roof of his mouth a little for extra persuasion.

Horses do not have teeth between the front incisors and the back molars. (See figure 5-3) Instead, the jaw in this area is simply smooth gums, so you do not have to worry about being bitten.

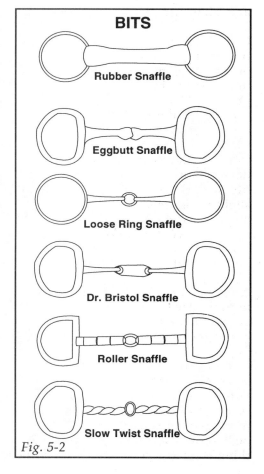

BITS

Rubber Snaffle

Eggbutt Snaffle

Loose Ring Snaffle

Dr. Bristol Snaffle

Roller Snaffle

Slow Twist Snaffle

Fig. 5-2

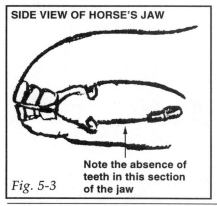

SIDE VIEW OF HORSE'S JAW

Note the absence of teeth in this section of the jaw

Fig. 5-3

When your Mini opens his mouth, gently push the bit into his mouth, while moving the top of the bridle over his ears. Try not to bang the horse's teeth with the bit, because this will cause him to toss his head. Move slowly and gently when pulling the bridle up the face, taking care not to poke the eyes with the straps or buckles. Again, it's important that experiencing new things is as pleasant as possible for your horse.

One trick to encourage your Mini to accept the bit faster is to coat it first with a little bit of honey or molasses; this makes it a more appealing and pleasant experience.

Once the bit is inside the horse's mouth, pull up lightly and finish buckling the bridle. Once that's done, you will need to adjust the bridle so that the bit fits properly. This is done by lengthening or shortening the bit adjustment straps. *(Refer to figure 5-1)*

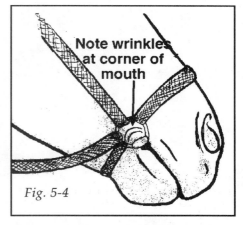

Note wrinkles at corner of mouth

Fig. 5-4

Correct placement of the bit in the horse's mouth will cause the corners of his mouth to wrinkle downward slightly. *(See figure 5-4)* To check that the bit is the right width for your Mini's jaw, place your index finger between the ring on the bit and the horse's face. Your finger should fit snugly in this space. If it is much wider, you will need a narrower bit.

After the bit is adjusted, leave the bridle on the horse for approximately 15 minutes. He will probably spend most of his time mouthing or "playing" with the bit. It is a good idea to have this first bridling lesson take place in the stall where the horse is familiar with the surroundings.

Have a daily session of putting the bit in your horse's mouth and leaving it for increasingly longer periods of time. At the end of the first week of practicing with the bit, your Mini should become progressively more relaxed and less resistant to having the bit placed in his mouth. Once he has worked up to 30 minutes or more and is not playing with the bit, you are ready to proceed to the next phase in his training. If you take each lesson slowly and introduce only one thing at a time, you won't need to spend time correcting bad habits later.

It is always a good idea to be on hand to handle any potential behavior problems, especially during these early lessons. Repetition is the key to training any horse. The more often a procedure is repeated, the faster the horse learns that this is a part of his life, like eating and sleeping.

During these sessions of acquainting the horse with the bit, use this time (as in halter training) to accustom him to some of the other devices he is going to meet later. While your Mini is in his stall, wearing the bridle, you can work on getting him prepared for some parts of the harness that you will need to use for ground driving lessons and hitching him to a cart. *(See figure 5-5)*

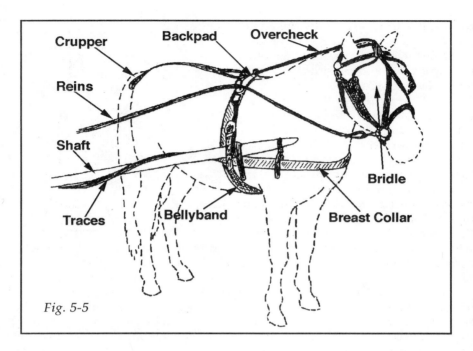

Fig. 5-5

HARNESS PARTS

If you proceed slowly, you can teach your Mini to accept several different new experiences at once. Never introduce something new if he acts the least bit concerned or starts misbehaving. Instead, stop and let him relax. In doing this, you will never betray your Miniature's trust and he will follow you anywhere and do anything you ask. This is a very special bond between horse and owner.

The following lesson will introduce your Miniature Horse to having something on his back. Start with a small, light-weight blanket, such as a crib blanket or lap robe. Show the blanket to the horse and let him smell it. If he looks unconcerned, rub him with the blanket, starting at his shoulders. Talk to your Mini in a soft and reassuring voice. Gradually work up to rubbing the horse all over with the blanket. Do not be concerned if you can't do this the first time; be satisfied if he smells it, which means that he is curious and interested.

When he stands quietly while you rub him with the blanket, try to place the blanket on his back. Always keep one hand on the blanket during these first lessons. You do not want the blanket to fall down around his legs and frighten him.

Eventually, the horse will learn that the blanket will not hurt him. At this stage, gently flap the blanket all around his body. This old-time procedure is known as "sacking out a horse." It prepares your Mini to accept something coming toward his body, especially things he has not seen before. Once he accepts this procedure, he is on his way to learning one of the most important lessons you can teach him: to trust you.

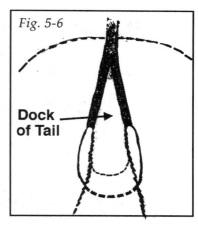

Fig. 5-6

Dock of Tail

Use the blanket on both sides of the horse. When he stands quietly for this, he is ready to go for the next lesson. Never throw or flap the blanket around your horse's head, since this can cause head-tossing, shying, or rearing.

Another piece of driving tack that your Miniature will need to accept is the crupper. *(See figure 5-6)* A crupper is a teardrop-shaped strap which is made of leather or rubber. This strap is placed under the horse's tail and keeps the harness from slipping forward. To prepare him, stand alongside him and lift his tail. Do this for several days until he is unconcerned. The next step is to lift your Mini's tail with one hand and place your other forearm under the dock of his tail, close to the buttocks. Ease the tail down onto your forearm. Don't forget to talk to your horse and reassure him that everything is all right. Repeat this process a few times, raising and lowering the upper part of his tail and placing it on your arm. The motion of lifting his tail and placing your arm under it will accustom your Mini to having a crupper under his tail.

When conducting lessons with your Miniature, keep them brief in the beginning, gradually increasing the lesson times. Horses can become bored or tired, especially young ones. You'll want to end the lesson before that happens. As your Miniature matures, the lesson times can increase. A well-trained and mature Mini can tolerate lessons up to two hours long. But even older horses become bored, and something as simple as changing where the lesson takes place is all that may be needed to whisk away that boredom.

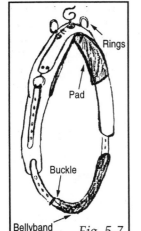

Rings

Pad

Buckle

Bellyband   Fig. 5-7

If you've handled your Miniature a lot, such as with daily grooming, the next stage of training will go much faster. The horse should now be used to being handled all over his body without becoming unsettled. This next stage in training Minis is simple because of their small size. It is easy to wrap your arms almost all the way around a Mini's belly. This will not seem like a lesson to you or your Mini—give your horse a "belly hug" a day! By doing this, your Mini will get used to pressure around his middle and these hugs will help make the introduction of the bellyband and backpad a much easier process.

By the end of two weeks, your Miniature Horse should be

accepting the bridle, a blanket, a hug-a-day, and his bit. It's now time to move on to two more pieces of tack: the surcingle or backpad, and the bellyband. *(See figure 5-7)* With the ends of the bellyband resting on top, place the surcingle on the horse's back about four inches behind the withers. This should not concern him if you have done your homework with the blanket. Now, take the bellyband (sometimes also called the girth) and run it under his belly near the front legs. Gradually tighten the bellyband. It should not be too tight, but tight enough that it will not slip.

Once it's on the horse, if he has a bad reaction, leave him in his stall with the equipment on until he becomes accustomed to it and settles down. Stay close by to talk to him, feed him some of his favorite treats and, otherwise, distract him. Once he's settled down, take your Mini to his usual spot for a short lesson while still wearing the backpad and bellyband.

If the horse shows no adverse reaction to this piece of tack, proceed directly to his workout. After his work session, bring him back and try to attach the crupper. Attaching the crupper could take a few days or weeks, depending on the horse. Some horses adjust faster, others are more sensitive. Know your Mini's limits and anticipate his reactions to new experiences.

Important: Do Not Rush This Part!

To begin, remove the bellyband. Move the harness back toward the horse's loins. Let the crupper hang down on top of his tail. Grasp the tail and pull it through until the crupper is resting between the dock of his tail and his buttocks. Slowly lower the tail onto the crupper. Letting the tail down too fast can upset your Mini. The underside of a horse's tail is very sensitive. If you drop the tail, the horse could bolt forward or start kicking to try to rid himself of the crupper. In the process, the backpad and bellyband could fall off and become entangled in the horse's legs. The key to this step is to move slowly.

If you have prepared your Mini by putting your arm under his tail, as demonstrated in earlier lessons, he should not object too strongly to the actual piece of equipment. Be sure to have a firm grip on the backpad and bellyband, should you need to get it out of the way in a hurry. Take your time. If the horse is acting nervous, then stop, remove the crupper, and go on to something that the horse feels comfortable doing. The time you spend teaching your horse to accept the crupper without a fight will be worth the effort.

When your Miniature is at ease with the crupper, re-attach the bellyband and backpad, then lengthen the crupper so that it hangs about an inch below the dock of the tail. Take the horse out to his work area and lunge him **at a walk only** until he has lowered his tail. Once he relaxes his tail, stop and check the harness and crupper. The crupper might need to be adjusted to keep the harness in place. A well-fitting crupper should give the horse about one inch of play between his tail and the crupper. A crupper that is too tight will cause irritation to the dock of the tail and one that is too loose will not hold the harness in the proper position.

When the horse is lunging normally (as he would without the harness and the crupper), it is time to stop the lesson. Unbuckle the bellyband and, keeping a firm hand on it, grasp the crupper with your free hand and gently slide the harness back toward the horse's hind legs. This will give you some slack to raise the crupper past the tail bone. Pull the backpad/bellyband off at the same time. Praise your Mini and give him a few extra treats, which are most definitely in order for his good behavior!

Horses have a long memory, both good and bad. If they associate treats for good behavior with harnessing, it is a good memory. If, on the other hand, they associate a bad memory with the harness, it could take weeks to correct. Or worse, the horse will never forget, and harnessing will always be an unpleasant experience for both of you.

Chapter Six

Ground Driving & Lunging
(Or, At the End of Your Rope?)

(C.Tunstall)

This chapter will take you through the steps needed to train your horse to the bit, through the proper use of ground driving, and to teach the gaits used in driving, whether for pleasure, show, or racing. At this point, your Miniature Horse is accustomed to most of his tack, including the bit, bridle, backpad, bellyband, and the crupper. The lessons that follow will introduce your Mini to more pieces of equipment and will show you how to teach your horse, through lunging, the subtle differences between a "collected trot" and a "working trot," and how to achieve a well-balanced "walk."

It is a good idea to introduce the cart to your Mini in the same way that you introduced him to the horse trailer. Place the cart where he can see it during his lessons, and walk him near enough to see the cart up close. Then, when you move it closer to the lesson area, he will not be concerned. Leave the cart in the lesson area while working your Mini. As you work the horse, take him closer and closer to the cart. He will become accustomed to it and will not fear it.

THE GAITS

To become good driving horses, Miniatures of all ages need to be worked at these gaits:
   "The Walk"
   Your Mini should walk actively with an even, four-beat gait, and display a calm demeanor.
   "The Collected Trot"
   This is the slower of the two trotting gaits and should be more collected. To understand the term "collected," picture a horse that looks "packaged," with his legs moving more up and down, rather than forward and out.
   "The Working Trot"
   This is a slightly faster-paced gait, showing an increase in the stride, with energy and impulsion. To determine if the horse is working at this gait, watch his hind feet; they should land in the footprints of his front feet.

WORKING ON THE LUNGE LINE

Tack up the horse with his backpad, bellyband, crupper, and halter. For now, you will not need the bridle or the bit. Attach the lunge line to the halter and begin the session with small circles, asking your Mini to move off at a walk. If he looks a little "strung out," cluck to encourage him to go faster in the walk, but without breaking into a trot. At this stage of training, the differences are subtle and it may take some time to teach the horse the difference between walking and walking in a nice package. You, on the other hand, will notice the difference when you see the horse make the desired adjustments. When you do, be sure to encourage this behavior and reward your Mini. Your tone of voice will play a big role in this process. Saying *"Good Boy"* as a reward, or using stern or sharp inflections when the horse is doing something wrong, is very effective.

Once the horse is walking at the desired pace, ask him to *"Whoa,"* congratulate him, and ask him to *"Walk"* again. Work your horse in both directions before moving on to the next gait. Now, ask for a trot, making sure that he trots at a slower pace. If he picks up a faster trot, say *"Easy"* in a soft voice to encourage him to slow down, while you tug gently on the lunge line. Once he has produced a nice forward moving, slower trot, ask him to *"Whoa,"* and again reward him with a few pats and praise.

Start the procedure all over again from the walk, progressing to the slower trot, and then "cluck" again to encourage him to trot faster and take longer strides, but without breaking into a canter. Use your lunge whip or crop if you need it to push the horse into the desired gait.

Once you have worked your Mini in all these gaits (in both directions), walk him around to cool him down. Never put a hot and tired horse away without cooling him down first. Be sure that his breathing has returned to normal. On really hot days, it is advisable to wash the horse or at least hose him down to remove all the salt, which can irritate tender skin.

GROUND DRIVING

Once your Mini understands the differences in the gaits, you are ready to proceed to the next phase: ground driving the horse. The previous lunging sessions have prepared your horse to work while wearing parts of his harness. During these next lessons, you will be adding the bridle, long reins, and the blinkers.

Ground driving differs from lunging in that, instead of the horse working in a circle around you, he will work with you following behind him. This will prepare him for the addition of a cart, carriage, or bike. At the beginning of this training phase, you should have a helper on hand to assist the horse into this very new experience.

Ground-driving your Mini helps him get used to working with all his tack. (T. Garman)

Train Your Own Mini

First you will need a set of long reins. (These can either be purchased ready-made or you can use long pieces of rope with clips on the ends.) Tack up your Mini with his backpad, bellyband, crupper, bridle, and bit. For the first lesson, use a halter over the bridle and attach a lead rope to the halter so that your assistant can help the horse understand your commands. Position your helper at the horse's head.

Next, attach the long reins to the bit, one on each side, and run the reins through the rings on the backpad. Take up a position 6 to 8 feet behind the horse and then gently raise and lower your hands so that the reins touch the horse. Ask him to *"Walk"* on a very loose rein. When you issue a command to the horse, your helper should move off at the same time. If the horse acts concerned, have the helper tell him to *"Walk"* while you walk along behind, gently encouraging him to move forward. Give your Mini all the time he needs to adjust to this new experience. Once he has moved off on your command, praise is in order for this very big accomplishment.

These first ground driving lessons should be conducted along a fence (or side of a building) to encourage the horse to move straight forward. If your Mini wants to move away from the fence, a little pressure with the rein that is closest to the fence will deter him and keep him straight. Progress slowly and always stop on a good note. Correct use of ground driving along a fence line will benefit the horse later and is essential in training the Miniature driving or harness racing horse. Once the horse has accepted having you behind him (which could take several days or even weeks), have your helper stand away from the horse and you try the lesson solo. At this point in the training, never ask for anything other than a walk. (It is not a bad idea to keep the helper close by in case you require assistance.)

Once your Mini is comfortable with you behind him and no one at his head, you can move on to the next step. One way to build your Mini's confidence is to break up these ground-driving lessons with lunging sessions. Alternate your sessions so that the horse is doing something he knows well one day and learning something new on the next.

During these ground-driving sessions, ask him to "whoa" frequently. At first, try to make him stand still for just a few seconds, gradually increasing this pause with each new lesson. This teaches him to stand quietly for longer periods of time—something that will be required during competition.

Always keep the horse walking forward in a straight line. If need be, continue to conduct your lessons alongside a fence. If you start in a clockwise direction, your lesson should end in a counter-clockwise direction. Keep the horse on a slightly loose rein. After the horse seems comfortable and is walking freely, apply slight backward pressure on the reins, stop walking, and say *"Whoa."* A little pressure goes a long way at this point in training.

STEERING YOUR HORSE

Keep in mind that it is a very new sensation for your Mini to have the bit pushing up, back, and down in his mouth. The bit applies pressure on the bars of the mouth and, in untrained hands, can be very painful. *(See figure 6-1)* You must make the horse understand that the bit is to guide him, not to hurt him.

How does this work? Simple. If he does not go in the desired direction, the bit applies pressure. The horse learns to remove the source of pressure or discomfort by turning with the bit.

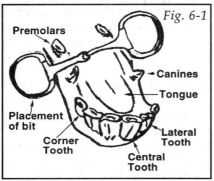

Fig. 6-1

Premolars

Canines

Tongue

Placement
of bit

Corner
Tooth

Lateral
Tooth

Central
Tooth

Start with the least amount of pressure and only increase it gradually until the horse moves in the desired direction. After a few lessons, your Mini should learn to move in the direction you want with only the slightest movement of your hands.

An important part of training any horse to the bit is what horse-people call having "soft" or "kind hands." Don't yank and pull the reins. Instead, use steady pressure. Hold the horse until he comes back to the pace or head set desired, then release pressure on the bit. Repeat this as necessary. If the horse does not respond the first time, apply more pressure and firmly give the command *"Whoa"* again. Having an assistant in these first lessons with the bit will help the lesson go more smoothly, simply by reinforcing your schooling. In this way, your Miniature will learn faster.

For these early ground-driving sessions, you have been using the rubber snaffle bit. Once your Mini understands and is accepting the bit and responding to your commands, you can introduce the metal snaffle bit. There are many variations of the snaffle, but you want your horse to perform using the mildest bit possible. A smooth, fat metal loose-ring or egg-butt snaffle is the most desirable. *(Refer to figure 5-2, page 34)* The difference between the two bits lies in the rings that attach to the reins. The egg-butt-shaped rings have less chance of pinching the horse's cheeks. But either type is highly recommended for the beginning harness driver, until they can develop their "hands" or sense of touch with the horse's mouth through the reins. A well-trained Miniature should be able to be driven in a snaffle bit even in his later years. Kind hands will be one of the best benefits of training for both you and your Miniature Horse.

Training a young horse can be both a delightful and frustrating experience. They have good and bad days, just like we do. Never let your frustration get the better of you or your Mini. Never yank on the horse's mouth. This will lead to head-tossing or a hard mouth that doesn't respond to the bit, thereby making the horse difficult to control.

CIRCLES AND TURNS

From his lunging lessons, your Mini should be accustomed to seeing a whip. Now it is time to introduce him to a driving whip. This addition lets you and your Mini get used to having both a whip and reins. After your Miniature has mastered the "walk" and "whoa" commands while ground-driving, you will teach him to move in a circle and to turn at a walk and a trot. As with the lunging sessions, you will work your horse in both directions.

To teach him to move in a circle with the reins, take up a position standing about two feet away from either his right or left hip. This will be the center of your circle. The side you are on will be the direction in which you want the horse to travel. One rein will come across the horse's back and the other rein will be on the inside of the circle.

As the horse starts to move around the circle, you can make it bigger by slightly increasing the pressure on the outside rein (the one across the horse's back). This will cause the horse to move his head outward and thereby increase the size of the circle. These beginning circle lessons with the reins should be done at the walk. It may take your Mini a few days or weeks to understand what is expected of him. Be sure to take it slowly and let the horse progress at his own pace. The time spent during this early phase in his training will be rewarded down the road.

Once he has mastered working in a circle while ground-driving, try to make a few turns at the walk. Go back to your position behind the horse and walk him along a fence or other barrier. As you come to a corner, apply pressure on the inside rein (the rein that is the farthest away from the fence or barrier) to make him move with the bit. At the same time, relax the opposite or outside rein to allow the horse room to move his head in the desired direction. Don't worry if he looks clumsy; all you are doing is teaching him to respond to the bit.

Unlike in the beginning, lunging circles and turns should be larger, rather than smaller. When your Miniature is attached to a cart, he will not be able to turn in a small area. Use your whole body when asking for a turn, plant yourself firmly in position, and make the horse move around you, with **you** being the center of his circle. In this manner, the horse will know what is expected of him. Your hands and arms should be an extension of the reins and always remain steady, regardless of what happens. Your hands should follow the horse's movements. If you've succeeded in using soft, steady hands on the horse, he will be more responsive to the slightest pressure on the reins.

FANCY STUFF

Your lessons should become increasingly more advanced. You'll be asking your Mini for a more extended or faster trot, and doing more complicated patterns, such as figure-eights and serpentines. Figure-eights and serpentines teach the horse to work off his back-end, which gives him more power and collection.

It is helpful for you to focus on a target while you are working the horse in circles or figure-eights. If you are looking at a cone, marker, or just a spot in the ground, your natural body movements will transmit through the reins. Soon, you will learn to feel the horse through the reins without looking. Once you achieve this connection to the horse, your hands and body move as one.

THE BIG BAD BLINKERS

Blinkers are the next piece of tack to be added to the equation. Miniatures vary with their response to blinkers. Some accept them easily, while others require more time to adjust. The only way to find out how your Mini will respond is to put them on him. It is a good idea to get your assistant to help you the first time you use the blinkers. The assistant should stand at the horse's head while you are holding the reins. As you give a command, the assistant can lead him off and make the process much easier. But before you proceed to the blinkers, make sure your Mini is ready and is responding to the reins, doing all the ground-driving lessons freely and easily, and listening to your hands and voice.

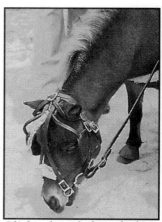
Blinkers keep the horse looking straight ahead (except when nibbling!) (C.Tunstall)

Horses have great peripheral vision. *(See figure 6-2)* Blinkers force them to concentrate on what is straight ahead and allow them to see nothing behind them. During the first lessons with the blinkers, you'll find out just how much the horse trusts you. Take it slowly. If your Mini shows signs of being nervous or stressed, don't try to ground-drive him. Instead, leave the blinkers on, use a halter either under or over the bridle, then stand by his head where he can see you. Ask him to walk around with you the first time. Pat his neck and say *"Good"* to reassure him. Keep the lesson short.

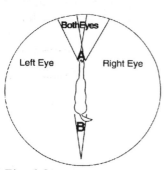
Fig. 6-2

Since he is not able to use his full range of vision, he will have to trust you to lead him. These lessons will reinforce the bond of trust between you and your Mini. If you rush the horse into work with the blinkers instead of allowing him to adjust to them, you'll always have a horse that is uncertain. Remember that what you are striving for is absolute trust.

If your Miniature shows no adverse reaction to the blinkers, then repeat all the ground-driving lessons in this chapter, this time using the blinkers.

MARTINGALES

Does your Miniature hold his head too high or too low during his lessons? There are pieces of tack that you can use to correct an improper head set or to give you more control of the horse's gaits through pressure on the bit. These are known as martingales. There are many types of martingales, but the one most commonly used is the running martingale. A running martingale is a very useful training aid. (See figure 6-3) This type consists of a Y-shaped piece of leather with rings on the ends of the "Y" that attach to the reins, and a loop of leather that attaches to the bellyband. This type of martingale is useful for training a young horse. It sets and applies downward pressure on the bit. If the Miniature tosses his head up, the running martingale will apply pressure. Once the horse discovers that it is uncomfortable, he will keep his head still and in position. The running martingale works better and faster than we can react. It also teaches the Miniature to "listen" to the bit and reins.

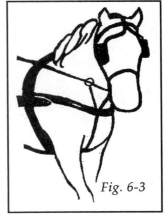

Fig. 6-3

A running martingale hooks over both reins.

As mentioned, there are many types of martingales, all providing different types of control. You'll find that experimenting with a few will give you a much better idea of what works best on your Miniature. All horses have different reactions and/or habits; what works on one may not work on another.

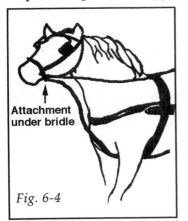

Attachment under bridle

Fig. 6-4

A standing martingale has a single strap attached to the bridle.

The use of the running martingale during training does not necessarily mean that you will have to use it in the future. Once the horse has learned to respond to the bit and the martingale, try taking it off and working the horse without it. Many times, when the horse has learned to respond to your hands and has accepted the bit, you can put the martingale aside.

PLAY IT SMART AND SAFE

When you are finished with your lessons, always remove the backpad and bellyband BEFORE the bridle. Without the bridle you have NO control of your horse. NEVER remove the bridle first, it should be the last piece of tack you remove and should immediately be replaced with the halter and lead line.

Clean your tack regularly. Salt from the horse's sweat can ruin leather. Clean the harness and bridle with saddle soap or a glycerin bar to remove sweat and dirt. The bit should be wiped off after each lesson.

Proceed slowly, taking each one of these training sessions in order. Your reward will be a Miniature Horse who is both willing and cooperative. Work at the horse's pace and learn what to expect from your Mini. Anticipating his reactions will help the process go faster and be more productive.

Chapter Seven

Hitching Up!
(Or, Save The Pieces!)

At this point in his training, your Miniature should be comfortable with all of his tack in place. Before you move on to this next phase of training, ask yourself these questions:

1. *Has he mastered the "walk," "trot," and "whoa" commands?*
2. *Is the horse at ease and moving freely with all of his tack?*
3. *Does he stand quietly at your request?*

If you can answer *"yes"* to all of the above, your Mini is ready for the next step in his schooling: getting acquainted with the cart.

MANY CHOICES

There are several different types of carts and buggies: show buggies, racing bikes, pleasure carts, and easy entry carts. Show buggies are generally made of wood and come in a variety of styles and sizes, depending on the type of driving or the number of horses pulling the vehicle.

A racing bike. (C.Tunstall)

Racing bikes and easy entry carts are also made of wood. If your plans include racing your Mini, the light-weight metal type is better suited to your needs.

Professional trainers usually use light-weight racing bikes to accustom the horse to pulling a vehicle. These are skeletal carts, designed for one individual, and having two rear- mounted bicycle wheels with wire spokes and rubber tires. When driving this type of cart, the driver's feet are up on the shafts of the cart.

Pleasure carts or easy-entry carts are also made of wood or metal and have the same two wheels. They also include a seat big enough for two people. Some may come equipped with a basket behind the seat, but all have a foot-rest or bottom that allows you to step up and into the cart before you sit down. The easy entry cart is a good choice to start your training. Although it is not as light, it is good for someone new to driving because it allows a more upright position in the seat, provides a basket for your feet, and places you higher up and farther behind

An easy-entry cart. (C.Tunstall)

the horse. Another reason to use the easy entry cart is that it will accustom the horse to pulling a cart with a little more substance. After your Mini has become adept at pulling this type of cart, the transition to a lighter cart will be a welcome change, instead of the other way around. If the horse has been trained with the lighter cart first, you may have to re-train your Mini to pull a heavier vehicle.

PUTTING THE CART BEFORE THE HORSE (so to speak)

You will need your helper for these first sessions with the cart. For your first lesson, tack up the horse, as in previous lessons, and take him over to the cart. If you left the cart where the horse was able to see it during his lunging and ground-driving lessons, he will probably not be concerned and show very little reaction.

Have your helper hold the horse facing the cart while you pick up the shafts and let them drop to the ground a few times. Be prepared! The first time the horse hears this noise, it might make him nervous, but, with your reassurance, he will come to understand that the cart is not going to hurt him. Be patient! It could take a few days or weeks to progress to the next step, depending on how often you worked your Mini in the presence of the cart in previous lessons.

Now change places with your assistant and have him or her pick up the cart shafts and start pulling it around the ring. Meanwhile, you will attempt to ground-drive the horse behind the cart. If the horse looks the least bit unsettled do not make him stay behind the cart! If he is looking at the cart with interest, you may continue, but always be ready to control him should the cart frighten him. He will probably be distracted by the cart in this lesson, so be patient and proceed slowly. If the horse acts nervous, keep him farther away from the cart, but gradually work up to having the horse walk closer to the cart.

Ask your Mini to stand quietly while your helper pulls the cart past him. Your helper should be watching the horse's reactions as closely as you, so that if the horse becomes upset, he or she can keep the cart at a distance where the horse feels safe. Once you or your helper can walk the cart by the horse without him shying or trying to escape, he has accepted the cart to be in his presence.

At this point, you will need to help him adjust to all the scary noises the cart can make. Whomever is pulling the cart should shake it as they pass, in order to familiarize your Mini with the sounds a cart makes while in motion. Remember, he won't be able to see it when it is behind him.

Now, with the helper pulling the cart alongside, ground-drive your Miniature until he is able to concentrate on his lesson. Remember to keep the cart at a safe distance at all times, in case the horse has a bad reaction. The last thing you want is to have the horse bang against the cart or, worse, become entangled with the cart. He will then be afraid of the vehicle.

Repeat these lessons until the horse has totally overcome his fear of the cart. If the horse is acting the least bit nervous, do not attempt to attach the cart at this time. Instead, work him until he shows no reaction when the cart is around him. This can be a matter of days or weeks, depending on your Mini, but the time invested in this familiarization project is essential to the success of your training program.

A LITTLE FIELD TRIP

If you are planning to race, it's a good idea to take the horse to a couple of racing events during this phase in his training. A Miniature harness-racing track is a good place to start. By allowing your Mini to have a good look around, you will introduce him to all of the sights and sounds that abound in a strange place. The more often you take him there, the better. Taking a horse to a strange place is a lesson in itself and, like all horses, he will learn to accept new things through repetition.

MORE DRIVING TACK!

Now, if your Miniature is acting calmly and has adjusted to the sight and sounds of the vehicle you are using, he is ready to be hitched up to the cart. Before you actually hitch the horse, however, there are a few more things you will need to know before proceeding.

Mini's are easier to harness than their larger relatives, mainly because the cart does not require the use of all the tack needed for the larger animals. What you will need is: the cart, the backpad/bellyband combination, reins, bridle, blinkers, shaft straps, harness straps, and thimbles. You can also use a breast collar, if desired.

There are two primary types of reins: flat reins and reins with handholds. Each type has its specific application. Flat reins, used for pleasure and show, should be held between the first finger and thumb of each hand, with your thumb on top of the rein. Your other three fingers should hold the reins into the palm of your hand. *(See figure 7-1)* This gives you the best grip and the most control. To give your horse more rein, all you have to do is let the reins slide through your fingers. If you need to take up some slack, put both reins in one hand, then make one of the reins shorter with your free hand. Alternate and repeat the process until the reins

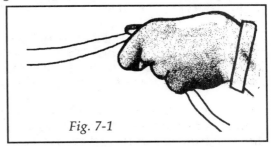

Fig. 7-1

are of equal length. Reins also help to reinforce your hand and verbal commands.

Reins with handholds are required equipment in sanctioned racing competitions. These reins have extra pieces of leather that form a loop for your hands and provide a better grip. (*See figure 7-2*) They are also advisable for training, because single reins of leather or nylon can slip easily out of your hands. The handholds

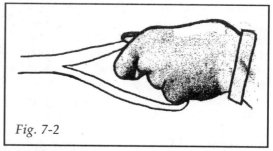

Fig. 7-2

give you more to grip and make it less likely that you will lose the reins. It's also a good idea to get used to wearing gloves for driving. Gloves provide you with a better grip and are required during racing events.

A breast collar has certain advantages: it gives the horse added leverage when he is pulling a cart and accustoms him to additional tack. The breast collar is a long strap that rests across the horse's chest and continues back along his flanks,

where the ends (called traces) are secured to the shafts of the cart. The breast collar is held in place by an adjustable strap that runs over the horse's shoulder in front of the backpad. Most Miniature harness-racers use thimbles instead of the breast-collar. Thimbles are tube-shaped pieces of leather that fit over the tips of the shafts; they act as brakes, keeping the shafts well behind the horse's

The breast collar provides more leverage for pulling the cart. (CTunstall)

shoulder. (*See figure 7-3*)

Both A.M.H.A. and A.M.H.R. require blinkers for show competitions. Martingales (either standing or running) are optional equipment and can be used, if needed, during driving classes in sanctioned Miniature Horse shows. (*See figures 6-3 & 6-4, page 47*)

TACKING UP, STEP-BY-STEP

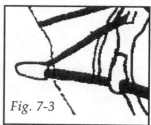

Fig. 7-3

The order in which your driving tack is put on your horse should go like this:
1. Attach the backpad and bellyband.
2. Attach the crupper.
3. If you're using a breast collar, this will be the next piece of tack you'll put on the horse.
4. Otherwise, you'll attach the thimbles to the backpad.
5. Put on the bridle.
6. Attach the reins. (Keep the reins in a big, loose knot to keep them out of the way.)

Now you're ready to hitch your Miniature to the cart. But first, ground-drive the horse long enough to warm him up, making sure you take him by the cart several times. On the final pass that you make, drive him past the cart on the left-hand side, and ask him to stop. Now, position the horse directly in front of the shafts of the cart. At this point, your helper should place a halter on the horse and attach a lead rope. Have the helper stand by the horse's head in case you need any help controlling him.

This handler carefully adjusts all the straps and buckles on the harness.

Checking the fit of the bridle and placement of the bit is very important. (C.Tunstall)

THE CART—FINALLY!

While your assistant holds the horse, the cart should be moved slowly up behind him. Be sure to stay "tuned" to the horse as you are attaching and securing the different pieces. As you work, talk normally to both your horse and your helper.

A helper is a very good idea when hitching up your Mini. (C.Tunstall)

If you're using a racing bike, you'll either have shaft straps or quick-release latches. Some harness racing trainers and drivers prefer the quick-release latches as opposed to the shaft straps. These latches provide the horse with more freedom of movement and, if the horse gets into trouble, enable you to detach the cart faster. The quick-release latches are attached to the shafts and then snapped into their counterpart on the backpad.

If you are using leather shaft straps, these are attached to the backpad and are wound around the shaft several times, then buckled to secure the shafts to the backpad. These straps are designed to hold the shafts in place and they can be adjusted to the proper height for your Miniature. Make sure the straps or latches are not too tight. They should be secure without putting too much pressure on the backpad.

Quick-release latches (above) and shaft straps (right). (C.Tunstall)

Proper fitting of the cart to your Miniature is

very important. The front portion of the shafts should be just above the large muscle over the horse's elbow. The tips of the shafts should not extend beyond the horse's shoulders. Once the quick-release latches or straps are attached to the vehicle shafts, the horse is "hitched" to the cart. Check the belly band after securing the shafts; sometimes it will need to be taken up a notch or two.

If you are using a breast collar, attach the traces to the ends of the shafts. The traces should have a little play and not be stretched tightly. If you're using the thimbles, slide them over the tips of the shafts. Again, make sure there is a little play in the thimble straps, but not so much that they will allow the shafts to travel past the horse's shoulder. Check the fit of all of the tack before you proceed with this session. Your Miniature is now harnessed to the cart. Take the reins and run them through the rings on the backpad and stand alongside the cart. Have your assistant ready at the horse's head.

Do not get into the cart at this point.

Your Mini will need to get used to the weight of the cart. This is something very new. Proceed slowly. With your assistant at the horse's head, ask the horse to *"Walk."* Your helper should encourage the horse to walk forward. The first turn

This handler is ground-driving his hitched up Mini as a warm-up. (C.Tunstall)

that you make with the horse and cart should be as wide as possible. Your helper will come in very handy at this point. When you ask the horse to turn, the helper should also turn at the same time; this will reinforce your commands. Keep your eyes focused on where you want the horse to go. As in lunging and your previous ground-driving sessions, be sure to give the horse definite signals so that he will understand what he is expected to do. Plant yourself firmly and your body movements will communicate to the horse the direction in which you want him to travel. (Don't forget to work in both directions.)

If, on this first lesson with the cart, you make a couple of wide turns and the horse is behaving calmly, have the helper move back to behind the blinkers, then continue on with your lesson. Continue walking, asking the horse to *"Whoa"* and *"Stand"* a few times.

Once your Miniature has accepted pulling the cart and is going along smoothly and willingly for you, it is time to prepare him for some added weight in the cart. At this stage in training, some trainers just hop in the cart and all is well. In keeping with the nature of this book, it is suggested that you add some weight to the cart before getting into it yourself. If the horse has a bad reaction and bolts, you could lose your balance or fall, and it will frighten him. He will *never* forget it. These situations can and should be avoided. If you proceed slowly, the

Train Your Own Mini

horse will gain confidence from you and you will have a willing and trusting companion.

Have your assistant close by, again holding the lead at the horse's head. Place a 50-pound sack of feed or bale of hay on the seat of the cart. Work the horse as usual for a few days, ground-driving him with this weight and then increasing the weight to two 50-pound sacks or bales over the next week or so. Once the horse is pulling the cart with 100 pounds of weight, he is ready for you, the driver.

ALL ABOARD!

Now comes the day for which you've been working. While your helper holds the horse, step into the cart as gently and quickly as possible. Once you are in the cart, sit quietly and have the reins ready to ask your Mini to immediately move off at a walk. Now the horse has to adjust to your shifting weight and movements. Humans have the ability to think and reason; we understand how things work by just looking at them and can usually know what to expect. When dealing with horses, remember that they do not think as we do. Instead, everything is a new experience. If you remember this, it will save you many hours of frustrating lessons.

When you ask your Mini to *"Walk,"* your helper should also walk alongside the horse's head. Keep this first session simple and short. Make a few wide turns, then ask the horse to *"Whoa"* and *"Stand."* Praise him for his good behavior.

Keep your helper around for the first two or three sessions with you in the cart. Afterward, the assistant should be close by in case you get into trouble, but otherwise, you can take on these simple lessons alone. As you progress, ask the horse for smaller circles and tighter turns, working him into progressively longer sessions.

Don't forget to vary your lessons. When the horse is not responding to your commands, ask him for something simple, and then quit on a good note. Pushing a horse that is tired or bored is a useless lesson. It also teaches him what he can get away with, instead of teaching him something productive.

In just a few weeks, your Miniature should be ready to move at a faster pace. Begin the lessons as usual; horses like to do what is familiar. Ask him to *"Walk"* and warm him up once in both directions around your lesson area. Now, ask the horse to *"Trot,"* slowly at first, and then encourage him to pick up the pace, still at a trot. Then, ask him to come back to a slow trot, and to a walk, and then stop. The only way to teach him to respond to your commands is to vary his gaits. For example, ask him to walk, then ask him to walk just a little faster, then bring him back to a slower walk.

Do the same thing at the trot. When your horse learns to respond to these subtle differences in gaits while harnessed to the cart, you are ready to begin putting the finishing touches on his schooling.

Chapter Eight

Finishing Your Driving Horse
(Or, So Much To Do, So Little Time)

Your goal is a nicely turned-out driving "package." (T. Leland)

This chapter will show you how to put the finishing touches on your driving Miniature. The goals here are to teach the horse to collect himself, to stand quietly and correctly, and to respond immediately to your commands. During these lessons, you will strive to keep the horse "on the bit" and to make him "work off his hind legs."

Horses are like people: they will pick the easiest way to accomplish a task. "Working off his hind legs" gives the horse more power and control, and makes for a much prettier picture. But, it is also more work for him!

To start, hold the horse with the reins, using constant pressure (don't pull) and, at the same time, ask him to move forward. This technique keeps the horse in a tight package and encourages him to use his back legs to push off, rather than using his front legs to pull him forward.

Remember to "give and take." When the horse yields his head to your hands, let up the pressure just a little to let him know that he gave the desired reaction. If he starts to look "strung out" and his nose comes up, take up on the reins again. Your Mini will soon learn to hold his head at the desired angle and use the power in his hind legs.

THE "HALT"

Your horse's next lesson will be the "halt." The "halt" is different than asking your Mini to "whoa." When asked to "halt," the horse must stop as quickly as possible in a balanced stance, much like in a halter class. When you ask your Mini to stop, you do not want him to take eight or ten steps before he finally executes your command. Instead, concentrate on stopping him in two strides. Since he will have to change his stride from a trot to a halt, two strides are acceptable.

When asking for the "halt," apply a little firmer hand and, with authority, ask your Mini to *"Whoa,"* or *"Halt."* Which word you use doesn't matter—it is the tone of your voice, combined with the command you give with your hands, that provides the result.

Don't be in a rush! It will take a few tries before your Miniature will understand what you expect. Start by asking him to *"halt"* within 8 or 10 steps, then down to four, and then two. Take your time. If he is not responding to your command, there is a way to teach this without using excess pressure on the horse's mouth. Drive the horse in a straight line directly toward a fence, building, or other obstacle. Wait until you're about six to eight strides away, then ask him to *"Halt."* Continue to ask him to *"Halt"* this way, shortening the distance between the Mini and the obstacle each day, but never less than four strides. With the obstacle blocking his forward motion, he will stop shorter to avoid hitting it.

BACKING UP

The next lesson will be to teach your horse to back up while he is hitched to the cart. Hitch him WITHOUT the blinkers for the first few lessons, so that he can see where he is going. School him as usual, only now you will incorporate backing into his lessons. It is helpful to have your assistant available the first time you ask your Mini to back up with the cart. The person standing at the horse's head can encourage him to move backward with the added weight of the driver and the cart. This is a new experience for your Mini, so you should proceed with patience and kindness.

If he takes one small step backward, pat him and praise him. Then ask him to walk forward. Repeat this a few times during your lessons. During these sessions, ask your horse to take a few more backward steps each time. When your horse is taking at least four steps back and is willing and responsive, you can put the blinkers back on him. Remember that, with the blinkers on, he cannot see what's behind him; instead, he is depending on you to guide him.

During each lesson, do not ask the horse to back up more than a few times. Horses do not like to back up. In the wild, a horse will avoid trouble by going forward. Backing up is unnatural to a horse. The horse should learn the command, but at the same time it should only be used when necessary.

Some Miniatures will use backing up in order to avoid carrying out commands. The only way to discourage the horse from backing up without your command is for the horse to associate backing up and walking forward as one, as described in Chapter Two. If taught properly, the horse will learn that when he backs up he is expected, in almost the same motion, to go forward. While hitched to a cart, the horse backing up without your command can lead to serious trouble, so correct your Mini immediately when he does this.

At this stage in your Mini's cart training, he should be doing figure-eights and serpentines at a walk, trot, and extended trot while hitched to the cart. If you have a friend or trainer who is willing, ask them to come over and drive their horse with you. This will be a valuable lesson for you and your horse. Your Mini will learn to pass and be passed by another horse and cart, and it will help you learn to judge distances when passing.

In the beginning, when practicing with another horse and driver, give your horse a lot of room to pass the other cart. Never go directly in front of, or cut off, another horse. If you are meeting another driver head-on, the rule is to always stay to the right.

Your horse needs to become accustomed to working in different environments and it is helpful to take the horse out of the lesson area. Start close by, but take him away from his usual area. Here he will see things that he is not used to and you will be driving a more animated animal. The horse will enjoy the change and be more alert to his surroundings. But remember, that almost anything can stimulate or spook your Mini: dogs, people, kids on bikes, cars, bags, puddles, and many other hazards (real or imagined) can cause the horse to become frightened. On these excursions, you must be constantly on the lookout for Horse-Eating Boogers! Be prepared to take action and keep control of your Mini.

During these outings, use trees to practice doing circles and serpentine patterns. In the lesson area, you can practice with cones to fine-tune your horse's execution of commands and your driving abilities.

PROBLEM SOLVING

Every horse owner develops his or her very own style of driving and uses these personal methods, to varying degrees, on all their horses in training. But sometimes it is necessary to be flexible and change your training to suit the individual horse. The ability to recognize that what works for one horse does not necessarily work for all of them is the sign of a good trainer.

Let's use bits as an example. You know that all horses should be started out in the mildest bit possible. As you train your Mini, you'll want to experiment with different bits to find the one that works best for him and requires the least amount of effort on your part. First you would try a snaffle bit with a smaller diameter that will apply slightly more pressure on the bars of the horse's mouth. If the horse does not respond to that bit, you would try a different type. If the horse holds his head too high, you might want to use a bit that encourages him to lower his head. Or, if the horse likes to try to get away from the bit, a standing martingale could correct the problem. Only through trial and error will you find the bit or piece of equipment that works best on your horse. Even after trying all the different types of bits, you may find that the one you started out with was the best one for your Mini.

OFFICIAL REQUIREMENTS & REGULATIONS

When planning to participate in any association-sanctioned shows, it is very important that you obtain and study a copy of the rules and regulations concerning specific events in which you are interested. Miniatures are required to use certain pieces of tack in sanctioned shows. Horses competing in driving classes in AMHA-sanctioned shows are required to wear either side checks or over checks and blinkers, and the driver must carry a whip in the show ring. In an AMHR-sanctioned event, sidechecks or overchecks and whip are optional equipment, but blinkers are required. In both AMHA and AMHR shows, Miniatures in driving classes are not allowed to wear boots or leg wraps of any kind. In both organizations, your horse must be at least three years of age to compete.

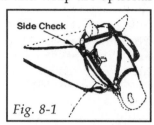

Sidechecks are small strips of leather which run from the rings on the bit, alongside the horse's jaw, and up to the top of the headstall, then down to the backpad. Sidecheck straps allow the horse to hold his head at a natural angle. *(See figure 8-1)*

Fig. 8-1

Overchecks are used to prevent a horse from holding his head too low. This strap runs down the center of the horse's face. It is attached to the noseband of the bridle and runs to the back of the headstall and then down to the backpad. *(See photo)*

(C.Tunstall)

PLEASURE, ROADSTER, OR OBSTACLE?

Before competing at a show, you should know the different types of driving classes that are offered. Your association rule book is an important source of information, in this respect. What follows are a few examples of the classes offered at AMHA and AMHR events and some of the requirements for each. (This is by no means a complete list, nor does it contain all the rules and regulations.)

PLEASURE DRIVING

Miniatures competing in pleasure driving classes always enter the ring at a collected trot in a counter-clockwise direction. All Minis competing in pleasure

classes are required to execute three gaits: a walk, a collected trot, and a working trot. Horses will be shown going in both directions of the ring, clockwise and counter-clockwise. Always keep your horse "on the rail" as much as possible during any driving class. If you do need to pass another horse, give yourself and the exhibitor you are passing plenty of room, then get back on the rail as soon as it is possible.

(C.Lekstrom)

In AMHR classes, all pleasure driving vehicles must be of the two-wheel type and have a basket. For AMHA, all divisions of pleasure classes may have both two- and four-wheel vehicles. Other pleasure classes for both organizations include Country Pleasure, Formal Park, and Viceroy. Country Pleasure is shown only in two-wheel carts, while Formal Park and Viceroy are shown in four-wheel and fine-harness carriages. Viceroy and Formal Park driving classes are for Miniatures that can deliver a brilliant performance with manners and elegance. The trot displayed in Viceroy or Formal classes should animated and high stepping, yet light and without excessive speed. In these classes, the overall appearance of the driver and the horse will be a consideration in the judging.

ROADSTER

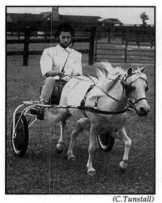
(C.Tunstall)

Roadster classes are limited to bikes, racing carts, roadster carts, or two-wheeled carts with stirrups and no basket. Drivers are required to wear stable colors or *silks*, with matching caps and jackets.

During these classes, the trot is the principal gait. Miniatures will be asked to perform three distinct gaits, all at the trot: a slow "Jog" trot, a faster "Road Gait" trot, and a fully extended "Drive-On" trot. The horse must be able to execute each gait distinctly and make the transitions to the other gaits as smoothly as possible.

Both AMHA and AMHR offer other specialty driving classes which include Multiple Hitch and Draft Harness. Multiple hitch classes are for two, four, or six-horse carriages and are shown at a walk and a trot.

OBSTACLE DRIVING

In AMHA Obstacle Driving classes, the emphasis in on the Mini's "way of going" through the course, his manners, and performance. In AMHR, the classes are judged 100-percent on manners and performance. For both associations, there is a 60-second time limit for each obstacle.

Some of the obstacles you might encounter in these classes could include:
    1. Backing through or out of an obstacle;
    2. Driving or walking through water or a narrow passage;
    3. Picking up an object while sitting in the cart;
    4. Driving or walking over a bridge;
    5. Driving or walking a pattern; or
    6. Standing still while the driver walks around the horse.

Points are deducted for being "off course" as follows:
1. Skipping an obstacle;
2. Going the wrong direction over or through an obstacle;
3. Taking an obstacle from the wrong side; or
4. Not following the required sequence set forth for the course.

Preparing for the Driving (or Halter) Obstacle Class

If you'd like to compete in the Obstacle classes, you'll need to practice with your Mini to accustom him to walking through water, over boards, and through or around a variety of objects. The most important thing you can do in training your Miniature Horse for these classes is to show him everything you can think of, including things you know will cause a big reaction. One of a Miniature's favorite scary items is an umbrella. Leave an open umbrella near your work area. While you pretend it's not there, walk the horse near the object until he stops being concerned.

This Mini walks right over a crackling tarp. (M. Rodkey)

Repetition is the key to familiarizing the horse with the strange items he will encounter away from home. Some Miniatures are frightened by flying objects or sudden movements. One way to cure your Mini of this type of spooking is to tie long, flappy pieces of rags to the fence in the pasture. Soon the horse will become so accustomed to the flapping rags that he will not give them a second glance.

The best way to prepare the horse for a bridge is to place a board on the ground and ask him to walk over it. If your Mini won't take that first step, place his foot on the board and reassure him. As with trailer training, let him go to where he feels safe for a few minutes, then start over again. Once he adjusts to the noise his feet make on the wood, you are half-way home. Then you can construct a little bridge that is slightly elevated for him to practice walking over. Make the bridge large enough so that, if you want to show him in a Driving Obstacle class, it will be wide enough to accommodate the cart and he will get used to pulling the cart over it.

Experience is the best teacher and exposing your Miniature Horse to all types of situations will help prepare him for the show ring.

Chapter Nine

The Racing Edge
(Or, He Went Thattaway)

If you're headed for the race track, here are some final pointers to make the journey a little smoother.

Miniature Horses of any bloodlines can be trained for the track if they display athletic ability. Racing Minis are undergoing a change through the breeding programs instituted in the last few years. 1995 was a stepping stone in the evolution of the racing Miniature Horse.

With the increased interest in Miniature Horse racing, some breeders have experimented with crossing Miniatures with Trottingbred horses in order to give the Minis the desired action for which trotters are famous. In the 1995 foaling season, there were 13 foals born as a result of these cross-breeding programs. These horses, as well as their sires and dams, are registered by the International Miniature Pacing and Trotting Association (IMTPA) in Littlestown, Pennsylvania, and will be known as Harnessbreds.

A "mini pace car" leads the field. (C.Tunstall)

For harness racing, your Miniature Horse will have to become acquainted with the starting gate. Before each race, the Minis line up behind a small truck or car that has a metal starting gate attached to the rear. (This is similar to those used for large horses, only on a miniature scale.)

Florida Miniature trainer Gina Vitek uses a golf cart for this phase of her race training. She puts a little feed on the back of the cart so that the horse associates the cart with food. Soon, the Mini is following the cart whenever it comes around. Gina gradually increases the speed of the cart, working the Mini up to a fast trot. In this way, the horse learns to follow a moving vehicle and this helps him adjust to the sight of the starting gate.

NECESSITY IS THE MOTHER...

If you do not have a golf cart, you can use your driving cart or carriage to get the same result. Racing bikes are light-weight and easy for you to pick up and pull around; pleasure carts have the added advantage of a basket in the back—a perfect place to put a bucket filled with a little grain. However, you can also make it work with your racing bike, with a little inventiveness on your part. Although you won't be able to keep the horse trotting for long, this will accustom your Mini to following a vehicle.

Once you and your Mini are at the track, your horse will probably follow the lead of the others participating in the race. Horses are herd animals and will stay with others of their kind, if given the opportunity. Use this herd instinct to your advantage when introducing your Mini to the starting gate. Encourage your horse to move forward, while staying slightly behind several of the experienced racers; your horse will follow them to the gate.

CONDITIONING

Racing Miniatures require extra conditioning to prepare them for harness racing events. Respected Texas trainers Jim & Arlyn Story use the conditioning schedule that follows. They recommend that you start this training regime at least three months before attending your first race. During the training season, your Mini should be worked six days a week, with one day of rest.

To begin, start the horse with a light-weight cart, such as a racing bike or pleasure cart.

Jogging daily conditions your Mini for racing. (C.Tunstall)

On Day One, do a jog-trot for 1½ miles.
On Day Two, increase the distance to 2½ miles.
On Day Three, jog-trot for 1 mile, walk the horse for one minute, then ask the horse for an extended trot over a straight course for one-quarter mile. This will accustom the horse to trotting faster on the straight-away or backstretch during a racing event.
On Day Four, jog-trot the horse for 1½ to 2 miles.
On Day Five, jog-trot the horse for 2 to 2½ miles.
On Day Six, jog-trot for 1 mile, build up speed for the next one-eighth mile, ask for more speed on the next one-eighth mile; then, walk the horse and ask for the faster extended trot (also known as the *sprint*) for one-eighth mile.
On Day Seven, rest the horse.

Gina Vitek's training program is a five-day-a-week regime that allows the horses to rest for two days during the week. At the beginning of the training season, she starts them off at a slow trot and works each horse for only 30 minutes on each of the five days. As the horse develops muscles and stamina, she increases the time and the pace, eventually working them up to a three-mile course at a fast trot. She also incorporates hills into the training program to build muscle during these workouts.

WORKING ON THE TROT

You want to encourage your Mini to trot as fast as possible without breaking into a canter. Horses that break from the trot are disqualified from winning a race. Work the horse at the trot until you know he is going as fast as he can without breaking into a canter. When dealing with horses, it is essential that you know the animal's limits. Hold

This Mini racer is really steppin' out!
(C.Tunstall)

your Mini back if you suspect he is going to break the trotting gait. As with all other training we've outlined, the only way to do accomplish this is through repeated practice. The horse must understand that he is not to change the gait, only the pace of the gait. When training to race, never encourage your horse to canter. You are training a trotting horse. Push the horse to a faster trot, but always be ready to pull him back if you feel he is going to break the pace.(Occasionally, you will find him cantering around the pasture, playing with pasturemates or just burning off excess energy. This is okay.)

Soon you will develop a feel for your horse. You will know his limits and know when you are pushing him past those limits. Horses have days when they are at their peak and days when they just don't want to do anything. You need to be aware of how your horse feels. Is he having a good day or a bad day? If you try to push him too much on one of his bad days, your Mini will try everything in his bag of tricks to avoid the work. On good days, the horse will do everything you've asked and then some. Hopefully, your horse will have a good day on race day, but if not, there are other days and no one, including your Mini, can always feel at the top of his game.

After each training session, always walk the horse around until he cools off and his breathing returns to normal. Hose him down, paying particular attention to his legs and chest. A liniment such as Absorbine can be used to limit soreness.

Once the racing season is underway, exercise your Mini five days a week; you will probably be racing once during the same week, so reserve the seventh day for rest.

After the racing season, your Mini should be turned out to pasture and not exercised until two to three months before the start of the new racing season. Everyone needs a vacation!

FEEDING THE RACING MINIATURE

Miniature Horses that race, like all athletes, require energy. You will need to supplement your Mini's diet during the racing and training seasons. Although it is best not to feed a Mini too much food, especially when they are not doing any vigorous work, you will need to provide him enough food to keep him in top condition and provide him with the stamina he will need to perform. Based on conversations with several racing trainers, the agreed-upon feed/weight ratio for a Miniature Horse in race training is: one pound of feed per hundred pounds of body weight. For a Mini that is just out to pasture, feed half or, preferably, less of that amount. Some trainers supplement their feed with different vitamins and minerals. It is also advisable to have a salt and mineral block available in the horse's pasture or stall at all times.

These delightful little horses are prone to over-eating and this can have dire results. The best advice is to consult your veterinarian about a feeding program designed to fit the needs of your individual horse.

OFF TO THE RACES!

The thrill of the race, with the wind flying around you as you speed around the track, blazing a path for the finish line, is fun and exciting! And you'll need to be prepared with some special equipment and dress for this great sport. During

And they're off! (C.Tunstall)

all competitive harness-racing events, drivers are required to be properly attired; this includes safety helmet, racing silks, white pants, and eye protection. Proper equipment is also required; drivers must have reins with handholds and the carts must have wheel covers. Whips are allowed, but cannot exceed 42 inches.

Miniature Horse harness races are broken down into two divisions: Shamrock and Hamiltonian. The Shamrock division is for Miniatures of 34 inches and under and the Hamiltonian is for Miniatures of 34 to 38 inches. There are both youth and adult races within the same divisions. The associations and Miniature Horse clubs have broken racing events into these divisions in order to give everyone, regardless of age, an equal chance to compete and win a race.

The field will be competing on a one-quarter mile track, with the starting gate positioned at the end of the back stretch. Drivers and horses are allowed to enter the track to warm up prior to their race. The announcer will tell the drivers when to take their horses to the starting gate. Once all the horses are behind the starting gate, it moves off just like on any other trotting horse track. Just before the starting/finish line, the gate moves away from the horses. As in other races, the first horse across the finish line is declared the winner.

WHO CAN PLAY?

Most harness racing events have 8 to 10 races on the schedule. You may compete with one or more horses in as many races as are available in your class. Classes during a racing event are also broken down into non-sanctioned club races, IMTPA-sanctioned races, age divisions, and height restrictions. There may be four classes in which adults may compete in either club races or races sanctioned by the International Miniature Trotting & Pacing Association (IMTPA), in addition to the different Shamrock and Hamiltonian divisions. The same holds true for the younger drivers. Children over the age of six and under 16 years old may compete in the club and IMTPA-sanctioned Youth races in the same Shamrock and Hamiltonian divisions. Children under the age of six are not permitted to race.

Winners in IMTPA-sanctioned races win points toward competing in the National Stakes Race. Although this big event is hosted annually at different tracks, Miniature Horse harness racing clubs come from all over the nation to compete for prizes, or *purses*, that can climb into thousands of dollars!

Miniature Horses must be aged three years or older to compete in the National Stakes Race. However, you may race your two-year-old horse in three races during the horse's second year to qualify it for the stakes race. A young Mini is allowed to attend two regional qualifying races to gain entrance into the National Stakes Race. If the horse is successful in winning both qualifying events, he will go head to head with other horses who made the cut in your region and will be eligible to compete in the big event.

All sanctioned races must be conducted according to the rules and regulations of the International Miniature Pacing and Trotting Association (IMTPA). There are many Miniature harness racing clubs in the United States that hold races in conjunction with IMTPA events. For a race to be sanctioned with IMTPA, the track must meet all criteria of the association. Your Miniature Horse must be registered with this association to compete in IMTPA events. Results of these races, along with recorded times, become official records at IMTPA headquarters, in Littlestown, Pennsylvania.

Racing is fun for all ages. (C.Tunstall)

FUN FOR ALL

The name of the game is F-U-N for all, no matter what your age. Miniature harness racing is a do-it-yourself, family-oriented sport. You and your children can train a Miniature Horse more easily and more quickly than a full-sized horse. Their diminutive size and calm, flexible disposition make handling them very easy; but, never underestimate their strength! Minis may be little, but they are still strong.

If racing is your dream, keep in mind that winning isn't everything at these events. The cameraderie and cooperative atmosphere is a bonus in this aspect of owning and enjoying Miniature Horses. You will find that the

(C.Tunstall)

paddock area is a beehive of activity, with children and their parents bustling around, preparing for races. Even grandparents get into the act, tacking up their Minis and hitching them to carts. Everyone lends a hand with putting on numbers or fixing a piece of equipment.

(C.Tunstall)

NOT AN ARM AND A LEG

Getting involved in Miniature harness racing is slightly less expensive than showing the horse in pleasure driving classes. For one thing, you can use the same cart to train and race without the additional expense of a show carriage. You can expect to pay approximately $350 for a used cart or bike, or $750 and up for a custom-made cart. Racing harness ranges from $75 for used equipment to $375 for new leather tack. A set of silks will cost $65 to $85 and the racing helmet runs around $60. Total startup cost can be kept under $1,000, excluding the cost of your Mini.

Regardless of why you decide to take up Miniature Horse Harness Racing, with a solid basis for learning and your well-trained Mini, you will have started a very enjoyable adventure. And who knows?

This could even be YOU!

Gina Vitek and Tonya Carter celebrate their victory with "SC Sweet Leah."
(C.Tunstall)

Appendix

Wit & Widsom From the Author

(Or, Everything I Ever Needed To Know, I Learned From Horses)

In my life-long love affair with Miniatures and larger horse breeds, I have gained a pretty good insight into the nature of horses and have developed a few techniques and tricks of my own. I would like share these with you; some you'll find funny and entertaining and others will be helpful and useful things to know.

Ever since I can remember, I wanted a horse; however, I was 16 before I took my first riding lesson. This first experience with horses was at an old, broken-down stable located next door to a speedway. I figured any horse that was accustomed to the noise of a Saturday night demolition derby would be as "boob-proof" as you can get!

That was my first lesson—a horse will become tolerancetolerant of anything if he is exposed to it for a period of time—even the roaring thunder of race cars behind the barn. When I purchased my mare, she had been living in a pasture next to a landing strip for small planes. As the planes landed and took off, she never raised her head from the grass. What this tells me and you is that the horse is a very adaptable creature.

A few years later, I saw a lovely little chestnut colt and promptly purchased him while he was still with his mother. On weekends I would go to visit him. What I learned from "Hot-Shot" was everything you don't want to know about a high strung colt! He had an endless bag of tricks. I was kicked, bitten, and stepped on. One day he took me for a drag, literally ripping both heels off my boots!

It was then that I learned not to fight with a horse physically. It is a battle you will never win. Use your mind to get the horse to do what you want, rather than brute strength. If the horse pulls away from you, go in the direction he is pulling.

Teaching a horse to load into a horse trailer, using my tehcnique in Chapter 3, can prevent a lot of pain and suffering for both you and your Miniature. When I finally got "Hot-Shot" loaded to take home, he arrived looking like he had been in a war with a can of gentian violet! Apparently, he had some reservations about getting into the horse trailer. The breeders had never worked with him near a horse trailer. This shows you that it can be dangerous to both you and your horse if he is not taught to accept the trailer. They are never too young to learn—as a matter of fact, the earlier the better. My youngest "trailer student" was a two-month-old foal who followed his mother into the trailer and was an angel for a two-hour ride.

My debut into the show world was at the bottom in a halter class. My first show was a disaster! My horse took a poke at the judge with his hind foot, but thankfully his aim was off.! However, I never consider anything as a failure, but rather as a learning experience. What I learned that day was that the person showing the horse needs as much training and experience as the horse they are taking to show. Practice makes perfect and the more you do anything, the better you become.

As the years passed and I got a little older and wiser, I learned to read how a horse "feels," through his movements and his stance. When horses are concerned, they take a very alert pose, ears up, and hindquarters tightened, ready to flee if necessary. If they are only interested in something, the stance is similar, but their muscles and overall body position are more relaxed. The only way to learn to interpret his thoughts is to pay attention to your Mini.

A happy horse moves willingly and freely. An unhappy horse will be tossing his head—a good indication something is wrong with his bridle or halter. Tail-wringing is a sure sign that your horse is not a happy camper! When something is bothering your horse, try to find out what the problem is first. If you don't find anything, then try distracting the horse. This is easily done by stopping what you are doing and scratching a favorite spot to relax him, or by showing him something new. Another sign of being upset is when the horse pushes at you with its head. This can be painful if you don't listen to what the horse is telling you. Playing head-butt with a horse is not a game for humans! Find out what is causing the horse to be anxious or upset, and try to remedy the situation.

One of the most common complaints by horse owners is not being able to catch their horse. I've found that you can teach any horse to come to you if you find the one thing they REALLY like. You can use food, but I don't advise it, because you might be some place where there isn't any food available. When I purchased my Miniature gelding, *Nikki*, I had a terrible time catching him. But Nikki loves to be brushed and I soon learned that he loved the brush more than he hated being caught. Now all I have to do is walk out with a brush in my hand and he races to the fence and waits.

The last and most important lesson that I've learned over the years is that all horses behave or react to each situation differently. One example is the first time that I took Nikki out in a cart with a neighboring Miniature owner. I was a little nervous, as it was our first time out with the cart in an unfenced area. Normally, Nikki would spook at bags and other items that blow in the wind. I saw a large, black plastic garbage bag and thought "Oh, No! He's going to bolt!" He surprised me by not even giving it a second look. The older, more seasoned Mini did spook at the bag, and my darling Nikki looked at him as if to say, "*So what's the problem?*" These situations teach you never to assume anything with a horse, but to always be prepared to take action, if needed.

Miniatures are wonderful and delightful animals and we are responsible for their well being. Always treat your Mini with the same respect that you would expect for yourself. Never ask him to do something without preparing him and never get angry when you have not prepared the horse properly. Getting upset transmits to the horse through your body language and your hands. The horse will then know that he is in control of the situation and take advantage of you. Always remain the dominant one and try to figure out the problem before reacting.

Playing the dominant role with horses is very important. Sometimes, like children, a Miniature will test you to see how far they can push before they get a response. Be sure that, if this happens, you take action firmly and immediately. The horse will then learn that you are in control.

Last, but not least, it helps to think like a horse. Horses, like people, have a pecking order. I know you fellas won't like this, but the boss horses—whether domestic or in the wild—are the girls! Granted, the stallion does most of the bossing, but when he approaches a mare, she then becomes the dominant horse. In a pasture full of mares, the most dominant mare will be in command because every herd has a leader. In the wild, the stallion leads the herd, watches for danger, and protects his mares.

Studies conducted by equine behavior researchers on domestic horses have produced interesting results. In one test, the researchers placed one stallion, one mare, her filly, one colt, and one gelding in a pasture together. They placed a large pile of hay in the center of the pasture and waited. The first horse to approach the hay was the stallion, but when the mare showed her displeasure, he retreated and waited at a safe distance. When the filly approached the hay, the stallion let her pass by and the mare tolerated her presence and allowed her to eat. When the colt tried to approach the hay, the stallion warned him away. The stallion reacted the same way with the gelding. After the mare had eaten and left the hay, the stallion ate and he allowed the colt to approach, as well as the gelding.

All horses need be assured they will not be harmed or abused and the person in control is you. Once they trust you, then you are the "boss horse." They will come to depend on your judgment in any situation, even doing tasks they would never do on their own.

If you want your Mini's respect you will have to show the same respect for his well-being. Be kind, be tolerant, and never push your horse to do anything he is afraid of. Once you learn how he thinks, you can anticipate his reactions.

A friendship will be formed between your Miniature and you, and this will give you a sense of accomplishment, along with a sense of pride in your Miniature's new abilities. But most of all, both of you will be happy. No one said it better than Will Rogers: *"The outside of a horse is good for the inside of a man."*

The History of Miniatures

The history of Miniature Horses can be traced back to the 16th and 17th centuries. All Minis evolved from the light horse breeds and, in most cases, the pony breeds—especially the Shetland. Miniature Horses are known to have existed in England and Northern Europe as early as 1765. During that time, they were used to pull carts out of the mines. Their small size allowed them to fit easily into the mine shafts and they were strong enough to pull the ore-laden carts. During this era, royal families kept the tiny horses as pets and playthings for their children.

Miniatures were introduced into the United States in the 19th century. Here they were used for the same purpose of pulling carts in the coal mines of Virginia and Ohio. Today's Miniature does not have to work at such taxing labor, but, instead, is enjoyed around the world as a pleasure driving horse, a harness racing horse, a show horse, or a pet.

About The Registries

Almost all Miniature Horses are registered in one or more registries. There are two main registries in the United States: The American Miniature Horse Association (AMHA) and The American Miniature Horse Registry (AMHR)—a division of the American Shetland Pony Club & Registry.

The American Miniature Horse Association (AMHA) was founded in July, 1978 to organize and promote the breed and maintain a permanent registry for Miniature Horses of 34" and under.

Another organization, the American Miniature Horse Registry (AMHR), was formed by the American Shetland Pony Club to complement the first association, and to allow the larger Miniatures up to 38" to be registered. The AMHR allows registration of horses in two height divisions: "A" and "B." Miniatures registered in the "A" Division are 34" and under; "B" registered Minis are 38" and under.

A third registry, the Falabella Miniature Horse Registry, is the oldest registry for Minis. These somewhat rare Miniatures originated in Argentina and are descended from pure horse strains, not ponies. This registry accepts only Fallabella-bred animals.

Racing Miniatures began as a randomly-scattered sport, but eventually four Texans decided that they would form a racing registry with bylaws and racing rules. Jim and Arlyn Storey, Arnold Gurley, and Betsy Harms contacted the

International Trotting & Pacing Association for help. Their goal was realized in october of 1992 when the International Miniature Trotting and Pacing Association (IMTPA) was founded. This organization provides services including computerized records and racing results on Miniatures and sanctioned tracks.

Other registries for Miniature Horses include The Canadian Miniature Horse Registry, Classic Miniature Horse Registry, World Class Miniature Horse Registry, and Universal Miniature Horse Registry. Information regarding these registries can be obtained by contacting them directly. (See Contacts)

Unlike other horse associations that issue a full registration certificate at birth, Miniatures (which are registered according to height) receive a temporary certificate at birth. For both the AMHA and the AMHR, both the sire and dam must be registered Miniatures with that organization in order for a foal to qualify for registration. AMHR and AMHA have different rules governing when the permanent certificates are issued. AMHR issues a permanent certificate after the horse has reached his 3-year-old birthdate. Miniatures registered with AMHA will not receive a permanent certificate of registration until they reach the age of 5 years and, as noted, they remain at 34" or under in height.

Things to Know When
Purchasing A Miniature Horse
(Or, Buyer Beware!)

When purchasing a Miniature Horse, take your time about making your decision. Don't let a pretty face or adoring personality steer you in the wrong direction. If you know a friend or someone who is knowledgeable about horses, ask them to go with you to look at the horse. Browse at several farms. Finding the right horse takes time, and a rushed choice often leads to a bad purchase.

Miniatures range in price from $400 for a pet-quality animal to tens-of-thousands of dollars for a top quality breeding stallion. While the horse that costs $400 might be the perfect horse for you, be aware that it is probably lacking in some way—either conformation, action, or breedability—that would normally cause the price to be higher.

Mares and quality stallions are usually more expensive than geldings or foals. A mare can return her purchase price several times over by producing foals. Stallions can generate money through stud fees. Pricing of Miniature Horses depends on these and other factors such as color, conformation, and show or racing records.

A first-time buyer's best bet is a gelding. As a rule, geldings tend to be more calm and they usually already have some training and are used to being handled.

Foals are usually the least expensive to purchase, but you will make up for it with money spent in training the horse. Plus, you could find that the horse is not suitable once it has matured. With mature Minis, you will get a more realistic picture of what you are buying.

Show horses and breeding stock can be very expensive. In these cases, you will want to purchase a Miniature with the best possible conformation that you can afford. It is possible to combine the best of both—pleasing disposition and great looks—but most breeders of these horses know what they have, and the prices will reflect that. Stallions with calm personalities, good conformation, and/or unusual color will be priced fairly high. These attributes are highly desirable characteristics that are often passed along by the stallion to his foals. A good stallion is vital to a solid breeding program.

If you are considering purchasing a Miniature Horse for your child, you will want an older animal with a pleasing disposition. Take the child along and let him or her interact with the horse. Watch the behavior of the horse around the child. When looking for a Mini for very young children, you want a horse that is safe, and displays a pleasing and calm personality.

Anyone interested in harness racing will want to consider a few more details. A newcomer to the sport will want a horse already trained to pull a cart. If you don't know what you are doing, it is essential that the horse knows! If you are purchasing a racing Miniature, have the seller hitch the horse to a cart while you watch. The horse should stand still and accept the tack and vehicle without resistance. Once the cart and harness are in place, watch how the horse responds to the driver. The Mini should execute all of the driver's instructions willingly and smoothly.

After conformation, behavior is probably the most important requirement when looking at a horse for the first time. If the horse is ill-mannered, don't think that you can change his habits after you buy him. It takes an experienced horseman to change bad behavior patterns and, even then, sometimes these patterns cannot be changed.

No matter what kind of Miniature you are hoping to find, always handle the horse yourself to make sure that the horse shows no resistance to your touch. Before handling any horse, here are a couple of things to know.

Many horses shy at being handled around the head and ears. This is very common, so do not let this interfere with your decision to purchase the horse. Most novices mistakenly approach the head first. Start by touching the horse on either the neck or shoulder to get acquainted. Don't automatically reach out to pat the nose.

The movements of the horse's ears are another good indication of his disposition or mood. If the ears are fully upright and alert, the horse is curious and attentive; if they are half-turned back, the horse is checking out what is behind or to the side of him. Ears flat back against the neck are a sure sign of an impending kick or bite.

The last, and most important, point when purchasing a Mini is to make certain you are getting what you bargain for. The seller should be willing to show you the animal's papers. Since Miniatures are a height breed, their size is very important. They can "go over" the height requirement and, therefore, not be registerable. The horse's papers will show the horse's markings for identification, the date of birth, breeding, and registration number. Beware of any seller that is not willing to show you the horse's papers, no matter what the excuse. While some excuses are (or at least appear to be) legitimate, the papers are your only guarantee that the animal is a purebred Miniature Horse.

Contacts

American Miniature Horse Association
5601 South I H 35W
Alvarado, TX 76009
(817) 783-5600

American Miniature Horse Registry
6748 Frostwood Parkway
Peoria, IL 61615
(309) 691-9671

Classic Miniature Horse Registry
600 Lee Road 23
Auburn, AL 36830
(334) 821-7741

Falabella Miniature Horse Registry
PO Box 36
Gettysburg, PA 17325

International Miniature Trotters & Pacers Assn
CR #381
Rockdale, TX 76567
(512) 446-RACE

Miniature Horse Association of Canada
R. R. #1
Holstein, Ontario N0G 2A0
(519) 334-4007

Universal Miniature Horse Registry
PO Box 6018
Sisterdale, TX 78006-6018

World Class Miniature Horse Registry
Rt. 4, Box 189
Vinton, VA 24179
(703) 890-0856

Sanctioned Harness Racing Clubs & Tracks

Appalachian Miniature Harness Racing
Falabella Downs, Gettysburg, Pennsylvania

Contact: Tom Cashman
32 Bonnie Heights Road
Gettysburg, PA 17325
(717) 334-9208

Blue Ridge Mountain Harness Racing Club
Shiloh Downs, Mt. Airy, North Carolina

Contact: Ronnie Clifton
1437 Airview Dr.
Mt. Airy, NC 27030
(910) 789-5922

Central Georgia Miniature Harness Racing Club

Contact: Bobbie Depew
Rt. 2, Box 2500,14 Road Ln.
Hawkinsville, GA 31036
(912) 783-0811

First Texas Miniature Harness Racing Club
Brazos Valley Mini Downs, Bryan, Texas

Contact: Jim or Arlyn Storey
18481 Elm Creek Rd.
Moody, TX 76557
(817) 853-2806

Florida Miniature Harness Racing Club
Bo-Bett Raceway, Reddick, Florida

Contact: Gary or Tonya Fleming
12006 N. Magnolia Ave.
Ocala, FL 34475
(352) 867-8474

Northwest Miniature Harness Racing Club

Contact: Christine Boggs
60 Harrison Rd.
Selah, WA 98942
(509) 697-5093

Glossary

amateur — A novice, or beginner who engages in a sport for pleasure. A non-professional.

Arabian Horse — The oldest pure breed of horse in the world. Foundation line of all the light-horse breeds. Arabian horses have one less vertebra in the back. Are known for their dense bones, stamina, beauty and the ability to pass on these characteristics.

arena — A contained or fenced-in area where you train or show a horse.

backpad — A piece of padded leather that rests on the horses back. Part of a harness for a horse to pull a carriage, bike or cart.

backstretch — The portion of a racetrack farthest from the grandstand and opposite the homestretch.

barrel — The section of the horse's body, behind the shoulders and before the loins.

bars — The part of the hoof wall where it becomes two wedges at the rear of the hoof.

basket — A metal/wicker basket found at the rear of easy entry carts.

bellyband or **girth** — The part of the backpad, that attaches underneath the horse to secure the backpad.

bikes — Two wheeled vehicles used in Roadster Classes or racing Miniatures.

blinkers — Two square-shaped pieces of leather located on the bridle that sit on either side of the horses head to force their vision forward.

bit — A metal or rubber device attached to the bridle and placed in the horse's mouth. Used to control the pace and direction as well as the horse's headset.

body brush — Short bristled, tightly packed brush, used to remove surface dirt.

boot — A wrap or supporting aid used on the fetlock of a horse's leg to prevent injury or add support during work-outs.

breeder — The owner of a mare or stallion where a horse was bred.

breast collar — A piece of tack used in harness driving. The device fits around the horse's chest and enables it to pull the weight with less effort.

bridle — A series of leather straps consisting of headstall, bit and reins. Fitted on the horse's head, it is used to guide the animal.

bridle path — The section of the mane that is clipped for the bridle or halter, located from the poll on the horse's head backwards approximately four inches.

buck — When a horse kicks out with his back legs and its head is lowered.

canter — A three-beat gait, that leads with one of the front fore legs, depending on that lead was asked for by the handler.

carriage — An elegant four-wheeled horse-drawn passenger vehicle.

cart — A two-wheeled horse-drawn vehicle used in either pleasure driving or racing.

cheekpiece — Part of the bridle, made of leather, attached to the bit and headpiece.

Coggins test — A test done on a blood sample taken from the horse to determine if the horse a carrier of EIA. (See Equine Infectious Anemia) Coggins tests enable a measure of control in the spread of the virus.

colic — Acute pain in the abdomen, caused by obstruction, gas or spasms.

colt — A young male horse less than four years old.

conformation — The symmetrical arrangement of the body parts of the horse.

contagious — The transmission of a disease or virus from one animal to another through direct or indirect contact.

coronary band — The area just above the hoof that is responsible for producing the horny tissue which is the hoof itself (much like the cuticle on humans is responsible for the growth of our fingernails).

crop — A short whip, usually used in driving or when riding a horse.

crupper — Leather or rubber strap looped under a horse's tail and attached to harness or saddle to keep it from slipping forward.

cryptorchid — A stallion with one testicle that has not descended into the sac.

dam — The female parent of a foal.

draft horses — The larger heavy-bodied horses such as Belgians, Percherons and Clydesdales.

equine — Term used to describe the entire horse family.

equine Infectious Anemia — Known as Swamp Fever; a virus transmitted by insect bites.

equestrian — A person who trains, rides, drives or is otherwise associated with horses.

ergot — The area at the back of the horse's leg behind the fetlock joint.

farrier — A maker of horseshoes, and one who shoes horses

figure eight — Two circles of the same size that join in the middle. Used as a pattern in training and showing horses at different gaits.

filly — A young female horse less than four years old.

foal — A newborn horse up to the age of one year. Can be either filly or colt.

forearm — The top of the leg that attaches to the horses shoulder.

founder — A term used to describe lameness, caused by swelling inside the horse's hoofs.

frog — Located on the underside of the hoof, this is a thick horny cushion on the sole of the foot.

gaits — Movements of the horse: walk, trot, canter, and gallop.

gelding — A male horse that has been neutered.

get — Referring to the offspring of the stallion.

ground-driving — Training the horse in full harness with long reins, but without a cart or bike. Used to accustom the horse to wearing his tack and learning his gaits prior to attaching the vehicle.

gelding — A male horse that as been castrated.

grooming — Cleaning the horse's coat and feet.

halter — A device that goes over the horse's face and is used to control the animal with the aid of a lead line or rope; can be made of leather or nylon.

hand — A horse term for a measurement that equals four inches; used in giving the height of the horse.

hard mouth — Referring to a horse that has been abused with a bit and has become non-responsive to the pressure applied by a bit.

hay — Dried grasses used for feed.

harness — All of the necessary tack used to hitch a horse to a cart or carriage.

headcheck — Straps of leather that run down the front of the horse's face and are used to give the rider or driver more leverage in controlling the horse's headset.

herd instinct — Horses prefer to be with other horses and will call out to other horses for reassurance or to sound an alarm. In a herd situation horses structure their rank much like in families. A stallion will be the protector and scout for danger, while his mares will tend to the foals.

hitching up — To harness a horse to a cart, carriage or racing bike.

hoof — Horny covering that protects the horse's foot.

hoof pick — Hooked metal tool used to remove dirt and other objects from a horse's feet.

imprint — In reference to horses, to bond and firmly implant relationships in the horse's memory.

impulsion — Movement achieved when a horse is collected and working off his hindquarters. It allows for distinct gaits and a higher degree of collection.

inflections — Changes in tone or volume of the handler's voice; a slight change of the horses movement or expressions.

in-gate — The entrance to the show area or ring.

inside rein — The inside rein is always on the inside of a circle or work area. (Example: If going around a ring in a clockwise direction, the inside rein would be the rein in your right hand.)

laminitis — Technical term for Founder. Inflammation of the sensitive laminae of the foot. Usually occurs when the horse has been fed to much grain, worked on a hard surface, or is overweight. Miniatures are very susceptible to founder or laminitis.

light horse — Any of the light horse breeds which include, but are not limited to, the following: Arab, Quarter, Thoroughbred, Paso Fino, and Morgan.

line-up — In a show ring, when all the horses stand for inspection by the judges, usually in the center of the ring.

liniment — A medicated liquid or cream rubbed on the skin for soothing sore, sprained or inflamed areas.

lunge line — A long piece of rope or nylon strap with a clip and chain.

lunging — An exercise used to teach a horse his basic gaits. Usually with a long line, the trainer directs the horse travel around the circle doing the requested gaits.

"made the cut" — When a horse is selected during a show to receive an award.

mane — The long hairs that grow from the top of the horse's head and down the neck.

manners — A well-trained horse that behaves and is easily controlled.

mare — A female horse. Usually at the age of four years.

martingale — running martingale: a "Y" shaped piece of leather with rings on the ends of the Y-pieces; used as a training aid by the rider/driver to gain more leverage in guiding the horse; standing martingale: a training aid used to keep a horse from holding his head too high, or for one that tosses its head.

Miniature Horse — A small breed of horse that, once full grown, does not exceed 38 inches in height.

monkey mouth — A conformation defect where the lower jaw is longer than the upper.

noseband — Part of the bridle that rests across the upper part of horse's nose, below the cheeks and above the bit.

oats — A cereal grain used as part of horse feed.

"off course" — Term used during a competitive event when you or your horses moves in the wrong direction over or around an obstacle, or out of the designated pattern.

"on the bit" — A term used for when the horse is holding the bit in his mouth and listening to your signals through the reins.

"on the rail" — At competitive events, to use the entire ring by staying as close to the outside of the area as possible without cutting into the center of the ring.

outside rein — The rein that is held in the hand that is farthest away from the inside of the area or ring you are working in.

overbite — Same as Parrot mouth; the upper jaw protrudes farther out than the lower jaw.

overcheck — A "Y" shaped piece tack, attached to the bridle, that is used to control the headset of the horse.

paddock — A fenced area.

parrot mouth — Same as overbite.

peripheral vision — The ability to see to the rear and to the side.

presence — A look and attitude that sets the horse apart from the others.

produce — Referring to the offspring of a mare.

propulsion — The use of the hindquarters to propel the horse forward.

poll — The very top of the horse's head between the ears.

qualifying race — An event or race that, if he places, allows the horse to compete in the final event.

Quarter Horse — One of the light horse breeds, with more powerful overall conformation. One of the distinctive characteristics is large hindquarters.

rail — The fence or barrier in a competitive arena.

reins — Flat pieces of leather that attach to the bit on the bridle and run back to the rider/drivers hand. Used to control and guide the horse.

safety helmet — An approved piece of protective head gear worn by drivers and riders.

sanctioned — An authorized or recognized event with specific rules and regulations governing the events and classes at a horse show, based on the approving organizations.

schooling — Training a horse to do a specific task or learn a required gait.

senior horse — Any horse over 5 years.

serpentines — A snake-like pattern used in training and showing horses.

"set up" — To ask or place the horse in the accepted stance during competition.

shying — When a horse moves suddenly away from an object.

shafts — Part of a carriage or cart. They are made of wood or metal and extend from the front of the cart and in turn are secured to the harness on the horse

sidechecks — Two strips of leather that run along the sides of the horse's face and attach to the bit. Used to set the horse's head and for leverage.

silks — Silk or woolen shirts, displaying the colors of the owner or farm.

sire — The male parent of a foal.

snaffle — The simplest and mildest bit which comes in a variety of types.

sprint — To run or race at full speed.

"square-up" — To stand balanced on all four feet.

stallion — A male horse, or four years or older.

stamina — In good physical condition meaning to be able to go the distance without fatigue.

stance — The proper posture with emphasis on the position of the feet.

"strung out" — When a horse is not collected and working off his front legs the horse appears 'strung out.'

supplement — A dietary addition to the horse's regular food.

surcingle — Also know as the bellyband; the piece of tack that goes around the barrel of the horse; the rest of the harness equipment is attached to this piece.

teeth — When fully grown, horses have 40 teeth, although female horses lack the canine teeth, or "tushes."

thimbles — Tube-like pieces of leather that fit over the ends of the shafts of a cart or carriage. Used as a brake and to keep the shafts from going past the horse's shoulder.

Thrush — A degenerative condition of the frog that is the caused by not cleaning the hooves regularly. It can lead to lameness.

traces — The ends of the breast collar that attach to the cart.

throat-latch — The area where the head and neck of the horse meet behind the jaw.

trot — A two-beat gait in which the legs move in diagonal pairs.

Trottingbred — A breed of Miniature, achieved by crossing the Harnessbred and the Miniature Horse.

twitch — A device used to restrain or distract a horse. Usually applied to the upper lip of the animal.

underbite — The same as Monkey mouth; the top jaw is shorter than the lower jaw.

walk — A four-beat gait, with the feet of the horse striking the ground in the following order; right rear, right front, left rear, left front.

"way of going" — The unique style in which each horse executes his gaits.

weanling — A term used to refer to a foal that has been taken away from his mother, usually at the age of six months.

wheel covers — Circular disk type covers that are placed over the spokes of wheel used on carts. These covers prevent equipment or other objects from becoming tangled in the spokes of the wheel. Required equipment in racing events.

whip — A tool that can be of varying lengths and is used as an aid in teaching a horse.

"work off the hind legs" — A term that defines a horse that is collected and using his hindquarters to provide his forward movement.

yearling — A horse that has reached its first birthday.

Bibliography

Paul, Stanley. Veterinary Notes for Horse Owners. 17th Edition, Simon & Schuster, 1968.

Stoneridge, M. A. A Horse Of Your Own. Revised Edition, Doubleday & Company,1968.

Credits

All illustrations, unless otherwise noted, are provided by Equine Graphics Publ.
Photographs by Cynthia Tunstall, with the exception of the following list:
Page 5, 6, 11, 12, 21, 28, 31: Lynn Ingles, Inglemist Miniature Horses, Sorento, IL
Page 11:   Pearl Perry, Vista Crest Miniatures, Elizabethtown, IL
Page 14, 20, 33, 60: Cheryl Lekstrom, Windcrest Acres, West Boylston, MA
Page 17, 30, 31, 57: T.M. Leland, Equine Graphics Publishing
Page 42:   Ted Garman, Holly Hill Farm, Lynchburg, VA
Page 62:   Melissa Rodkey, Aylett, VA

Additional Reading

Conformation
"Basic Foot Structure," by Michael Berluti
"The Importance of Straight Legs," by T.M. Leland
"Understanding Teeth," by Kenneth L. Marcella, DVM
The Miniature Horse in Review, Vol. 1, 1995, Small Horse Press

Driving
"Basics of Driving," by Ted Garman
"Buying Used Vehicles," by Bonnie Kreitler
The Miniature Horse in Review, Vol. 1, 1995, Small Horse Press
"Good Habits Mean Good Driving," by Bonnie Kreitler
Getting Started With Minis, 1995, Small Horse Press
Driving Digest Magazine, PO Box 467, Brooklyn, CT

Foal Training
"Bonding—Nature's Insurance Policy," by T.M. Leland
The Miniature Horse in Review, Vol. 2, 1996, Small Horse Press
"Raising a Well-Mannered Foal," by Kathleen Schubert
The Miniature Horse in Review, Vol. 1, 1995, Small Horse Press

Grooming
"Clip Art," by Bonnie Kreitler
The Miniature Horse in Review, Vol. 2, 1996, Small Horse Press
"How To Make Your Mini Shine," by T.M. Leland
Getting Started With Minis, 1995, Small Horse Press

Halter Classes
"Miniature Horse Classes At A Glance"
"What Are The Judges Looking For?"
Show Your Mini! by Toni M. Leland, 1996, Small Horse Press

Harness & Tack
"Buying Your First Harness," by Bonnie Kreitler
Getting Started With Minis, 1995, Small Horse Press

Index

About The Author

Writer and photographer Cynthia Tunstall is a winner of the prestigious Dudley Peebles Award for most outstanding photograph, as well as being the recipient of numerous awards for writing, best column, and best feature story, from 1986 through 1988.

Cindy cut her teeth on a rocking horse, according to her mother, and this was a sign of things to come. At the age of 16, Cindy acquired her first horse and so began an ongoing love affair with horses for the next 30 years.

Cindy and her husband, Jim, started their married life in Florida, raising and training Arabian horses for halter and performance classes. Cindy later moved on to the hunter divisions and some dressage training, thereby expanding her expertise in these fields.

In the ensuing years, Cindy became interested in photography and writing for regional, national, and international publications. Her love for horses inspired her to write for equine publications such as Equus and Western Horseman; she is the Florida correspondent for HorsePlay magazine published out of Gaithersburg, Maryland. Cindy provides information on the Winter Equestrian Festival in Florida and covers the American Invitational, which is the last leg of the "Triple Crown" of horse jumping competition—an event held yearly in Tampa.

Cindy's baptism into the world of Miniature Horses came almost 25 years ago, but a chance meeting at a recent all-breed show in Ocala showed her the remarkable changes in the breed. Captivated by a beautiful yearling Miniature, Cindy was inspired to find out all she could about the breed. To her dismay, she was able to find only a handful of information.

As the owner of two horses—one Arabian mare and one Miniature gelding—Cindy decided to write this book as her contribution to Miniature Horse owners, in hopes that it would provide helpful information for both novice and experienced Miniature Horse owners alike. And, in keeping with her deep feelings for horses, Cindy dedicates this book to her mare, Alieea, and Nikki, her Miniature Horse.